WOMEN AND RAPE

WOMEN AND RAPE

Cathy Roberts

Harvester Wheatsheaf

New York   London   Toronto   Sydney   Tokyo

First published 1989 by
Harvester Wheatsheaf
66 Wood Lane End, Hemel Hempstead
Hertfordshire, HP2 4RG
A division of
Simon & Schuster International Group

Printed and bound in Great Britain by
Billing & Sons Ltd, Worcester.

British Library Cataloguing in Publication Data

Roberts, Cathy, *1950–*
    Women and rape
    1. Great Britain. Crimes. Rape. Social
    aspects
    I. Title
    364.1′532′0941

    ISBN 0–7108–1214–0
    ISBN 0–7450–0639–6 (pbk)

---

1 2 3 4 5   93 92 91 90 89

CONTENTS

PREFACE

Since women began actively organizing against rape in the early '70s our battles have been hard fought and our victories have been few and far between. For those who have been involved in anti-rape organizing for several years, morale has often been low in spite of these victories.... Even after a self defense class or a speech with a responsive audience, the phones at rape crisis centers keep ringing, as though all our work were powerless to stop the agony of the women on the other end of the line.

('Feminist Alliance Against Rape',
September/October 1976)

Rape is an integral part of human history. In the development of mankind, rape has been used as a weapon both in mass conflicts and everyday battles. For womankind, women's bodies have been used, not only to inflict pain on, but as the weapon with which to defeat and humiliate the opposing males – the presumed real owners of those female bodies. This book has grown out of the history of the Women's Movement, and out of the experiences and lives of those women who set up and used the London Rape Crisis Centre. Feminist thought and actions are not often acknowledged as part of our society's heritage, but a part they are. Similarly, the work of the feminist Anti-Rape Campaign, and the personal experiences of women who have been raped, are a part of the background and development of therapy and support services the world over.

In looking at women's own responses to rape, it is helpful to explore the possible explanations of why rape occurs. What this book does not and cannot do is explain rapists. No particular biological or psychological type has been recognised as 'rapists' (other than men), but the search for a specific has dominated research in the past. Emphasis has been placed on abnormal use of aggression or sex by rapists compared with 'normal' men.

There is an immediate problem with this. Rape does involve both aggression and sex and therefore either would be likely to help provide a definition. But, both sex and aggression, even the combination, are accepted as normal and useful in male behaviour. Feminists, in explaining rape, looked not at the imprisoned rapists – the ones too ignorant, black, or insane to be ignored – but at normal, everyday male behaviour. This view came not from obtuse theorising, but from the accounts of raped women. The women whose accounts illuminate this discussion also showed that rape was not created from the abnormal, but came at them from normal, everyday situations.

Susan Brownmiller, whose book *Against Our Will* (Brownmiller, 1975) was a turning point for a published understanding of rape, saw that the development of mankind left womankind on the sidelines, as observers and occasional casualties. In truth, until the last two decades, we knew very little of women's experiences, except what was filtered through indirect sources. Information on the rape of women in wartime was not collected because of the hurt done to women but because it was part of the chronicle of male action. We could have learned directly from the women who had persevered and taken their assailants through the courts had anyone seen them, but we learned instead from police records and newspaper reports. We learned in effect what it was to be a rapist, not what it was to be raped. Because society's view was that women, like children, should be seen and not heard, and because as a society we are uncomfortable with victims, women who had been raped were silenced until a safe space could be found for them to speak.

That safe space came with the rise in the 1960s of the 'new wave' Women's Liberation. The Women's Movement in the US and Europe provided two unique factors which allowed rape to be seen in a new light. Firstly, women were questioning their own lives, challenging how experiences had been defined for them, and giving themselves and each other new explanations for unequal pay, rights and status. Secondly, the Women's Liberation Movement gave women the space to talk about their lives, encouraged them to see the value in each account. The experience, and the number of them, was a shock. The myth of the misplaced seduction, lying women and occasional real mad rapist was a social myth; the real pain of rape was as hidden from feminists as from the rest of society. Having opened the channels for the pain to be expressed, the next step was to do something about it.

The Anti-Rape Campaign began in the late 1960s/early 1970s and continues today. As well as providing the support services, the wider social movement also ensured that the accounts and views of women victimised by rape began to be heard by a wider public. Feminist support services, their approach to dealing with women in crisis and the expressed needs of the women themselves, have made major contributions to therapy, counselling and the provision of social services. The first Rape Crisis Centre was set up in the US in 1970, and in the UK in 1976. More than a decade later, we can now see some changes in police procedure and a greater sensitivity in the officers; the medical profession can discuss and provide treatment for women who have been raped which does not necessarily assume they asked for it; the newspapers and women's magazines will give sympathetic and informative coverage, sometimes. Few of the police officers, doctors and journalists will fully understand where their new found awareness came from – but it is from the Women's Movement.

The work which forms the basis of this book started as the research for a PhD in sociology. The reason for doing the PhD was to have time to spend on research into victimisation through rape and the start of the Anti-Rape Campaigns. The study period officially lasted from 1976 to 1981, a five-year period which marked the establishment of Rape Crisis Centres and Crisis Lines as accepted, useful and productive services for raped women. As a counsellor still working with women who have experienced rape, my study period will never really end.

The accounts of thirty women are used to illustrate the information gained through counselling and talking to women who have been raped. Each agreed to her story being used for research purposes, usually in the hope that her experience would provide some information which would be useful to other women. In using it in this book, I have changed some detail and tried to use the accounts in such a way that they neither give an indication of any individual's identity, nor illustrate a point in such a way as to seem to sensationalise the subject or the experience. Rape has for too long fed the warped imaginations of the pornography writers and the junk journalists. What is important in these pages is not the details of the act of rape, but the whole process of victimisation from well before the act itself, to the point where the woman herself can say 'it's over and I'm through it'.

If only we could be looking towards saying that as a society.

ACKNOWLEDGEMENTS

This book has grown out of work for a PhD in Sociology, at Essex University, which I undertook while a member of the London Rape Crisis Centre Collective. I could not have done this without the support and co-operation of those other women who started the RCC in London, and the countless women and men who encouraged me in the United States. I no longer have close contact with the London RCC Collective, and this book may not reflect the work they do now. However, they and the other RCCs around the country have strengthened the Anti-Rape Campaign, and continue to give support to thousands of women. For that, the women currently involved deserve thanks too.

I would like to say thank you also to Ken Plummer, my supervisor for the PhD; Gloria Levine who was, in 1978, working with the National Centre for the Prevention and Control of Rape in Washington DC; the Pregnancy Advisory Service in London who trained me as a counsellor; and my friends and family who have lived with this work as long as I have.

More than anyone else though this book belongs to the women who have trusted me enough to share their experiences, and who helped me in the hope that work such as this would help other women. For them, a very special thank you.

1 UNDERSTANDING RAPE AS VICTIMISATION

> Fie on the falsehood of men, whose minds go oft a madding, and whose tongues can not so soon be wagging, but straight they fall a railing. Was there ever so abused, so slandered, so railed upon, or so wickedly handled undeservedly as are we women?
>
> (Anger, 1589, in Goulianes, 1974)

Feminism is an intricate interweaving of feelings, ideas and experiences which have become a set of views on the situation of women. Both the differences between the views and the wholeness they have created need to be understood, because they reflect the odd and conflict-ridden position women have in this society – 'this' society here being a western, Christian-focused, white male-defined and -controlled, capitalist society. Whether we as individuals fit any or all those categories, they are the dominant influences on the social structures in North America and Western Europe today. The fact that women do not fit into at least one category is part of the problem for society: where do women fit in at all?

Feminism does not supply a single, uniformly accepted and understood party line on why or how women are treated as they are, or even what we should do about it. Feminism is a forum for discussion, consideration and action. Though there is diversity, there are some stable, connecting points.

Even opponents of feminism would accept the view that women may live in a separate social sphere from men – the 'domestic world' at least. The opposition would argue that this is beneficial to women and designed to protect them. One feminist view would be that women's best protection would be economic and social independence, so we could look after ourselves. Another would say that women really *should* be in a different world from men but a world controlled by women for women, having little if anything to do with the 'other' world of men. The common ground in feminism is that women's position in the social structure should be defined by us and not by men on our behalf.

Both the equal involvement and the separatist views are developments from an understanding of women's situation as disadvantaged. Feminism sees the political situation of women as containing the possibility of victimisation, because the seeds of victimisation are inequality and the vulnerability produced by disadvantage.

The campaign against victimisation through rape is only one in a long line of women's campaigns against vulnerability and victimisation through civil and social inequality. We tend to think of feminism as a new phenomenon and indeed the work and ideas described here are concentrated in the last two decades. But, when Juliet Mitchell called feminism 'the longest revolution', she was acknowledging the constant presence of women-centred action, even if sometimes we have been quieter than at others. If the focus is inequality, and the potential for abuse from men, then the Anti-Rape Campaign can be seen as a direct descendent of 'Votes for Women' – and Jane Anger.

Feminist concern for the victimisation of women forced very real changes in how we all see rape. Read any of the textbooks on criminology or sexual offences prior to the 1970s and the victim is rarely acknowledged, other than in the special field of victimology, where the relationship between the offender and victim is the real focus of concern. Any understanding of rape as victimisation, i.e. based on the effect of the act or the view of the object of the offender's action, only really developed with the rise of feminist debate and action. What we learned was how women had been silenced, how many had shared the experience of rape, and how those experiences differed from the image of rape which had been given.

In a world where maleness is assumed unless clearly stated otherwise (Dear Sir to an unknown; chairman regardless; mankind to describe all of us), it is easy to assume that there is only one viewpoint, but this is rarely if ever true. If an analogy is made with sport, the spectator will describe a different game from the players – and may wistfully express regret at not being able to be more directly involved in the action. The ball, the object of the action, would not describe a game at all. Where the situation of women is concerned, there are times when feminism is the voice of the spectator and times when the voice becomes that of the subject of men's action.

There the analogy stops, for in rape we are not describing a game. A woman who has been raped speaks as the person acted on. She describes the experience of victimisation and its results, not the intentions and experiences of the offender. Where rapists talk of sex, raped women talk of pain and violence. The difference is that rapists treat women like objects, and women take it personally.

WOMAN – SUBJECT OR OBJECT

> That man over there says that women need to be helped into carriages, and lifted over ditches, and to have the best place everywhere. Nobody ever helps me into carriages, or over mud-puddles, or gives me any best place! And ain't I a woman? Look at me! Look at my arm! I have ploughed and planted, and gathered into barns, and no man could head me! And ain't I a woman?
> (Sojourner Truth, speaking in 1851, in Schneir, 1972)

This idea of women as delicate flowers, too sensitive to stand up to the rigours of real life, was an image, created by a particular class, culture and economic structure which had an excess of wealth to maintain a non-earning group of women. It was not the real-life experience of the majority of women. This minority image led in turn to the use of women as decoration, with a hint at least of sexual availability. Such images are hard to avoid, as no advertising – cinema, newspaper, magazine or poster – seems able to survive without using women's bodies to attract attention or encourage sales. It was not the idea that women are or could be attractive which caused feminist concern, but that they should be nothing more:

> We do succeed when we make ourselves objects, outside ourselves, something we expect others to admire because we admire, and which we admire through others' admiration. But it is not us really. Narcissism is not really the love of self, because self is the soul, the personality, and that is always something quite different.... That beautiful object we stand in awe before has nothing to do with the

person we know so well: it is altogether outside, separate, object, a
beautiful image, not a person at all.

(Dennismore, 1970, p. 14)

The message in the women's magazines may have become more
subtle, but there is still a touch of the old line which urged
married women to look after their appearance, go regularly to
the hairdresser, keep up with fashion no matter what, or risk
losing their husbands to the 'girls' at work. Feminism merely
suggested that the women at home and the women at work could
be better off co-operating rather than competing for the
attention of men, but it didn't achieve wide appeal, particularly
among men. The conservative-minded, defending the simple
pleasures of man (page three, striptease and other pornography)
have always accused feminists of being 'killjoys', of envy at
being denied male attention, of misjudging something harmless
or even of positive benefit to men. Some women, fearful of losing
their special status as pets and caretakers, snigger along with
their menfolk at the 'unnatural' women who called the sexual
use of women plain exploitation. This renaming was the result
of listening to the experiences of women, whose words painted a
different picture from 'harmless good fun', who talked of the fear
induced by unwanted and aggressive male attention. We saw,
with the eyes of women who had been raped, the danger of
reducing women to objects to be used. For that is the action of
the rapist.

'Fashion' was another silly obsession of feminism, for what
harm could come from women indulging themselves in a little
fashionable uniformity – or should that be 'deformity'? Throughout history, there have been dire warnings of the health hazards
induced by fashions – wasp waists, pointed shoes, four-inch
stiletto heels, pierced ears and highly coloured hair. Other cultures demand that some women are covered completely, to contain their attraction, or see no problem or anything unusual in
the female body. Social reaction to women's bodies or appearance is connected with their class or status, and their relation to
men. In China, a sign of sexual attractiveness, social and economic status for men was, until the revolution, to have a crippled
woman:

> Beauty was the way feet looked and how they moved. . . . Perfect 3
> inch form and utter uselessness were the distinguishing marks of
> the aristocratic foot. These concepts of beauty and status defined

women: as sexual playthings, as sexual constructs.... Bound feet
were crippled and excruciatingly painful.... Hard calluses formed;
toenails grew into the skin; the feet were pus-filled and bloody;
circulation was virtually stopped.

(Dworkin, 1974, pp. 101, 107)

The 'new wave' feminism grew up in the era of the mini-skirt
and platform shoes, a lethal combination of revelation and
immobilisation. Attractiveness for women meant walking a
tightrope between offering a promise of sexual excitement and
maintaining distance, for the image says 'look but don't touch'.
A picture can provide distance between the image and the
audience. On the streets, the distance is more difficult to see
when catcalls and whistles turn into obscenities and aggression:

I was pushing Melanie in her stroller when I heard someone call 'oh
baby...'. For a second I thought he was talking to the child and then
the rest sunk in.... 'How'd you like a hot cock up your ass?' Out of
the corner of my eye I saw he was a nicely dressed business type in
his forties, carrying a paper and an attache case. 'My god', I thought,
'if his wife could see him now'.

(Meade, 1973, p. 87)

The connections between treating women as less than human,
as appendages, and sexual violence against women, was obvious
to feminists, but still seem too complicated for some others to
cope with. Certainly, the effects of being a sex object could be
more distressing than the image-makers would have us believe.

USING AND ABUSING FEMININE PASSIVITY

For a woman to be good, she must be dead, or as close to it as possible.
Catatonia is the good woman's most winning quality. Sleeping
Beauty slept for 100 years, after pricking her finger on a spindle.
The kiss of the heroic prince woke her. He fell in love with her while
she was asleep, or was it because she was asleep?
Snow White was already dead when the heroic prince fell in love
with her. 'I beseech you', he pleaded with the seven dwarfs, 'give it to
me, for I cannot live without looking upon Snow White'.
It awake was not readily distinguishable from it asleep.
Cinderella, Sleeping Beauty, Snow White, Rapunzel – all
are characterised by passivity, beauty, innocence, and
VICTIMISATION. They are the archetypal good women – victims
by definition. They never think, act, initiate, confront, resist,
challenge. Sometimes they are forced to do housework.

(Dworkin, 1974, p. 42)

One of the first lessons feminists learned when looking at rape
was that women's lives are 'catch 22' situations. To be accepted
as a 'good' woman was to be passive, always ready to look to a
likely man for leadership. The inability to defend oneself was
seen as a positive attribute of femininity, until a man took
advantage of that defencelessness, when the lack of resistance
was taken as consent. (I use the past tense here because it does
seem as if the 'passive to the point of catatonia female' is less of
an ideal for more of us in the 1980s than back in the 1960s – but
I may be wrong.) Some would argue a natural passivity in
women, though nature seems to be selective as to the status and
class of the women chosen to be passive in reality. Even in fairy
tales, the Good Woman either starts or ends up as a princess, not
a working woman like Sojourner Truth. Others would no doubt
agree with Rousseau:

> Even if it could be denied that a special sentiment of chasteness was
> natural to women, would it be any less true that in society their lot
> ought to be a domestic and retired life, and that they ought to be
> raised in principles appropriate to it? If the timidity, chasteness and
> modesty which are proper to them are social inventions, it is in
> society's interest that women acquire these qualities: they must be
> cultivated in women, and any woman who disdains them offends
> good morals.
>
> (Rousseau, quoted in Okin, 1979, p. 122)

What is important to an understanding of rape is not where
passivity, if it is for real, comes from, but the fact that we believe
in it, and that in planning rape, men will work on that belief. In
general social interaction, there are at least three ways that
passivity is used.

To begin with, there is *inherent*, or that idea of 'natural'
passivity, spelt out in the rules of the feminine gender model.
Look at any list of 'feminine characteristics' and it suggests a
quiet life with little dynamic activity or decision-making. Juliet
Mitchell, in her reading of Freud's work, makes the clear point
that, in Freudian terms, male and female can be said to: '... be
distinguished by the preponderance in one of active aims and in
the other of passive aims' (Mitchell, 1982, p. 115).

A more sociological, rather than psychoanalytic, approach
would be to say that the gender stereotypes act as a script,
providing a structure which gives meaning to social situations
and some guidelines as to how to act – the cast and character

descriptions at least. Women, on the whole, can be assumed to be playing supporting roles, as that is what is written for them. When it comes to acting with the given script (or 'life', to bring us out of the theatre!), what can then be observed is *interactive* passivity. Here, women put into practice what they have learned or have been brought up to see as correct, and others will react as if to a supportive, or developmental role. The conversations where women act as 'feeds' to men or assume an interested air while the conversation excludes anything to do with us at all are examples of interactive passivity. What was it *Jackie* Magazine advised me years ago? 'Listen intently, he likes nothing more than a Good Listener. If he's telling you what is wrong with the car, and you know more about engines than he does, don't admit it.' I've thought of that advice often, but rarely, since I learned to laugh at male egos, have I put it into practice.

Although both inherent and interactive passivity have some connection with actual female behaviour, the third type may have no connection at all. Because the idea of passive femininity is very strong, it can colour or change the meaning of a situation and mask women's actions. *Assumed* passivity means just that – whatever a woman has actually said or done, she will be assumed to have done nothing:

> Women constantly confront themselves with questions about giving. Am I giving enough? ... By contrast, the question of whether he is a giver or giving enough does not enter into a man's self-image. ... They are concerned much more about doing. Am I a doer? ... Most of so called women's work is not recognised as real activity. One reason for this may be that such work is usually associated with helping others' development, rather than self-enhancement or self-employment. This is seen as not doing anything.
>
> (Baker Miller, 1979, pp. 53–7)

It is the assumption of passivity which allows a society to describe a mother and housekeeper as 'not working', and allows a man to whistle at, comment on or touch a woman in the street. It is also the assumption of passivity which allows a man intending rape to maintain control of a situation and deflect any attempt by the woman to impose any other meaning or aim than his.

There is assumed passivity in the law on rape itself:

> The concept of consent as incorporated in the law on rape rests on one very basic assumption about the nature of female sexuality and

male/female relationships. The word consent implies passive agreement, acquiescence, to something which is done to us by others ... something which is allowed and in which the consenter takes no part. Consent carries no positive active idea of female initiatory and participatory sexuality.

(Rape Counselling and Research Project [RCRP], 1977, p. 18)

What passivity gives us in total is the background to victimisation, the denial of self control. The feminine model provides an idea of women as existing to be used, social situations can help set a woman up, and assumed passivity will both delete her will and provide the rapist with an excuse – he didn't notice she didn't want to, so it must have been OK. Alternatively, it may never cross a rapist's mind that a woman has any say in the matter anyway.

Nowhere is the use of passivity in victimising women more obvious than in the area of sexuality, where the real difference between male-defined ideas of female sexuality and women's own ideas led feminists to challenge 'common-sense' assumptions about rape.

FEMALE SEXUALITY OR THE HORIZONTAL ROLE OF WOMEN

After all, the sexual life of adult women is a dark continent for psychology.

(Freud, 1926, quoted in Williams, 1977, p. 25)

The feminist exploration of female sexuality was embarked upon with all the zeal of a crusade. It was seen as a discovery (or re-discovery) of a long-buried treasure, the graveyard being the morass of theories and assumptions which had fed common-sense understanding and created the stereotypes which women had been taught to use as mirrors of their feelings. The 'new' feminism took apart the words and concepts used in 'classical' works and compared them with women's experiences. There was comfort in the work which tallied, leading to expansion and the testing of new ideas. As earlier feminists had done, the pioneers dumped much of what they saw as mistaken, misinformed or manipulative:

The idea of penis envy is a male concept. It is the male who experiences the penis as a valuable organ and he assumes that women also must feel that way about it. But a woman cannot really imagine the sexual pleasure of a penis – she can only appreciate the social advantage its possessor has. What a woman needs rather is a feeling of the importance of her own organs. I believe that much more important than penis envy in the psychology of woman is her reaction to the under-valuation of her own organs. I think we can concede that the acceptance of one's own body and all its functions is a basic need in the establishment of self-respect and self-esteem.

(Thompson, in Baker Miller, 1973, p. 65)

In the US, the feminist search for a self-defined sexuality for women was part of a more general interest in personal development and growth. There was criticism of this trend from the Left, especially in the UK where feminism and socialism have a shared history not so clear in the US. The Left saw the preoccupation of feminists with sexuality and personal development as a distraction; a sign of the distance between the movement and working-class women or women of colour. Distance there was undoubtedly, but the criticism of 'middle-class indulgence' missed the point and the importance of the connection between the personal and the political. Feminism saw that the political oppression of women could not be challenged until its roots in personal life had been exposed and women given the chance to take control of their own lives and bodies. For those unable to imagine the effect of having their body legally owned and used by another, the debate on sexuality may seem still to be an indulgence. For the women concerned, it is a personal revolution. Women who had experienced rape could also see that the control assumed and used by rapists over them was no less important or oppressive than the effects of a totalitarian state.

Women began by turning a critical eye on the available social models for their sexual personality:

It was a big school with no yard. All the socialising took place in the halls which were literally meat racks. The first day I remember walking down the hall in a new sweater and a tight skirt.

During the summer I'd had a nose job. The boys kept looking at me and I thought, 'they're watching me. They think I'm attractive. Maybe some of them will like me'.

(Meade, 1973, p. 30)

There was a demonstration at the Miss World show in 1970:

I felt that the event symbolised my daily exploitation. I saw the contestants being judged by men, and I know what it feels like to be judged and scrutinised every day when I am just walking down the street.

(Wandor, 1972, p. 249)

In effect, the starting point was the male view of female sexuality, the public ownership of sexual attraction. This, combined with the private ownership of sexual gratification represented by marriage and the family, provided the first social understanding of female sexuality as existing to satisfy male needs. Even the much flaunted sexual revolution of the 1960s became less liberating when judged by women in terms of control over our own sexual pleasure. At a time when society was learning how to cope with sexually 'free' women, and men were learning new rules for good sex, women were faking orgasm. Gradually feminists began to see why:

> Thus, at the same time that radical feminists were being pressured by radical men to be 'good in bed' and always ready for it, they discovered sexual activity was not responsive to their own needs and desires. Women were not permitted to experience their own sexuality on their own terms. Her orgasm was important for *his* pleasure; bringing a woman to orgasm became a mark of a man's masculinity and virility. A woman's orgasm was seen as something he did to her or for her, playing her like an instrument; but the blame was hers alone if the music didn't come out right.
>
> (Coyner, 1977, p. 220)

In looking further, to the roots of a male-defined female sexuality, attention was drawn to what we see now as 'Victorian' ideals or morality. Although actually a time of considerable sexual freedom for well-off men, the latter half of the nineteenth century does seem to be a period where sexuality became a focus for critical attention, where the nuclear family (or bourgeois family) was glorified as an ideal, and where women both fought to become a part of the world and were trapped, by the family, in a world of their own. In essence, it was an age of contradicting absolutes which have endured to influence our thinking and acting today. The last hundred years has seen the whole area of sexuality become a major interest for psychology. Given the unreal idea of womanhood developed through the eighteenth century in Europe and the US, it is perhaps not surprising that women have suffered the translation of theory into practice.

Although put forward as an understanding of human

sexuality, the work of many of the classic writers was actually focused on male sexuality. Because this focus was unexplained, we now have a situation where neither male nor female sexuality is fully understood. What did emerge is an explanation of how an unequal, hierarchical society can create the conditions for a matching sexual interaction.

The first clarification of views which emerged from an investigation of sexuality was the idea of sex as a drive or force:

> While the right-wing sees sexuality as the demon within and the left-wing sees sexuality as the great liberator, both credit sexuality with enormous – almost mystical – powers in contributing to social order. Sex becomes the central force upon which civilisations are built up and empires crashed down.
>
> (Plummer, 1975, p. 6)

One line of thought saw an active sexual drive as belonging only to men, and the lack of such a drive in women as a natural and important inhibitor on men's sexual activity. The idea was that too rampant a sexual life would drain men's energy and distract them from the real world of commerce and empire creation. A seemingly opposite view was that women, in our natural state, were too sexual and not rational enough to cope with it. Women therefore needed to have this sexual drive trained out of us and then still be placed in the protection of a man who could contain and channel sexual energy into something more socially useful. Working-class and ethnic minority women, if considered at all, were seen to have had no such training and were therefore not entitled to male protection or concern. While Victorian 'morality' developed for the middle classes, the sexual exploitation of lower-class women grew apace.

In social terms, women were regarded as similar to children – in need of guidance and incapable of self control. The idea of a woman having the will-power to choose whether or not she wanted sexual activity was represented only as far as her refusing the advances of an unsuitable male (which she would do because a good woman would not desire sex). In all other ways, women's sexuality was seen as essentially passive, satisfied through male satisfaction, if the idea of pleasure or satisfaction came into it for women at all. Even the image of the 'enchantress' – a woman using her sexual desires to break down man's imposed control – is not that of a woman acting under her own control, but out of control.

For women, sexuality was very clearly linked with reproduction. The needs of procreation demand that sperm reaches the uterus, and the usual method of transport is by penis via the vagina. The separation of sexual pleasure from reproduction has been, until the last twenty years or so, only available to men. The new contraceptives, such as the pill or intrauterine devices, have given us the potential to share with men the separation of sex from pregnancy, which is exactly the objection the conservative-minded have to their use. It is interesting to reflect that vast industries now exist which are there to provide sterile intercourse. The less costly and simpler answer would be to encourage sexual activity which gives pleasure without penile penetration, but this remains unthinkable while sexuality is considered from a male perspective, and the majority of society sees vagina–penis intercourse as the only 'proper' sex.

The sexuality offered to women was, as with so many other areas of our lives, passive action. Women were expected to receive sex and to find gratification in pleasing men or in receiving sperm. There was an assumption that even pain would be received with equanimity if to give pain pleased the men in control. The actual experiences of women and the feelings expressed when looking at the treatment of their sexuality produced a less responsive view. Passive action is difficult to maintain and women acknowledged the subterfuge involved in 'playing' the ideal woman. The assumption of male control over sexual relations also meant that women felt that men often did not care whether a woman actually wanted or was enjoying sexual activity, and that there was no deeper reason for relationships than sex. The accounts of some women indicated that in addition to a lack of interest in a woman's feelings, men also showed a willingness to overcome any resistance and to force sexual activity.

The rules of femininity say that women should please men and always put their needs first. When acting this out, the rules further state that women should be seen and not heard. Add as a final twist, the possibility that men can ignore or dismiss what women say or do (like claiming 'no' means 'yes', or not hearing 'no' at all), and the potential for abuse is there. The ability of men to desire sex regardless or even in opposition to the feelings of women makes rape the form that abuse could take on. At root is an aggressive male and passive female sexuality.

The overall picture of feminine sexuality so far presented resembles a description of a clockwork doll – it would only work when wound up and the key holder had better be a suitable male. Feminism found another model which was based on women's needs and feelings, and was self-defined. 'The myth of the vaginal orgasm' (Koedt, 1970) was a paper known about by most feminists, though perhaps not that widely read. It asserted the value of the clitoris, over the vagina, in giving sexual pleasure and recognised the potential for a sexuality for women not defined by or dependent on men. Rather than an 'indulgence', a self-defined sexuality for women was seen as an essential self-defence and step towards full equality.

Though exciting and fulfilling in the gentlest of ways, the feminist quest for the perfect sexuality was also a war. The passivity of women was so well established as natural, or obvious or right and proper, that to challenge it was to appear to advocate chaos. The simple task of taking suitable precautions against pregnancy became an active search for sexual pleasure. A request for something different in love-making became a challenge to male domination and an attack on a delicate ego. A lesbian relationship is seen as a political statement about the value of men, giving strength to many lesbians and angst to many heterosexuals. Some progress has been made in the last few years, at least as far as the acceptability of an active female heterosexuality, but the faking and the conflict and the anger still goes on.

The passivity of female role models can be challenged, the worst consequences of a social understanding of female sexuality tackled, but when female and male sexuality meet the real trouble starts. Many women took the option of turning their backs on men and joining the women who had never wanted to look at men in the first place. However, for those feminists who had not given up on all men completely, working towards a self-defined sexuality and rejecting male definitions was only the first step. If relationships were to develop and progress into equality, then what happened in those relationships had to be looked at too, and men had to change into the kind of humans a feminist could live with.

FEMALE–MALE RELATIONS OR INEQUALITY INCARNATE

A popular conception of male and female has the two as (it is hoped) complementary opposites, the romantic myth being that, because female and male once shared the same body, then even separate, one is incomplete without the other. It is the lyrical explanation behind the strongly held belief that differences between the sexes are valuable and serve some purpose for society as a whole.

In philosophical, economic and political thought, the separation of domestic (home) life from everything else is obvious and so often unchallenged that it appears natural, taken as read. The male World and the female Home are studied as separate entities, and any deviation from the norm is commented upon. Men staying at home to look after children is seen as an unfortunate by-product of a shrinking job market or the castrating effects of Women's Liberation. The idea that some men may be happier in such a role than some women has hardly yet received serious consideration.

The overall picture presented is of a functional system where male and female roles are part of a well organised and regulated whole. In order to carry out their homemaking, breeding and rearing functions, Woman looks to the care and protection of the working, action-packed Male. The idea that men will have a protective instinct towards women is key to this cosy interdependency. Rape, an undeniable malfunction in this picture, cannot develop from the relations between male and female if they are in truth based on interdependence and protection:

> What is the middle-class American woman to do if her 'protector' refuses to support her or becomes abusive? Her dependency on him ... has probably become quite real as she has children and her ability to support herself diminishes. When she really wants to escape an abusive relationship, she may find that economically she is as effectively immobilised as the Chinese woman was by her bound feet.
>
> (Chapman and Gates, 1978, p. 19)

The intimate relationship between men and women in this society is very much tied up with the idea of the couple and the family. Conservatives or functionalists see necessary social benefits in these ideas and assume that a monogamous heterosexual couple best cater for and contain sexual activity, while the family is the only proper system for the effective rearing of children – inculcating them with the same views of society and their role in it. Radical positions concentrate rather on the economic relationships which form the basis of marriage and the family and how intimacy is reduced to a form of ownership. Love, we are told, makes the world go round, but we are told the same of capitalism. The acceptance of dependency by women has sometimes been called love, and so has the brutal imposition of authority by men. I once had a man explain his wife's fractured skull, and how he had given it to her, by saying, 'Sometimes, physical punishment is the only way to show you care'. Killjoys once again, we feminists insisted on looking at cosy domesticity and saying, 'well, yes, it does seem very nice, if it works out, but...'

For rape, the 'but' in the analysis of the intimate relationship is connected back to the separation of the sexes into two directly opposing 'ideal' models. Passive femininity is made vulnerable to abuse by aggressive masculinity. Because an intimate relationship is the last place abuse would be expected, when it does appear women are less prepared and therefore less able to oppose or avoid it. Further, the idea of the couple is based on ownership; the language of love is full of possessive phrases which mirror the economic and social structures. We used to believe that 'come the revolution' the world and our relationships would be changed for the better. For women with violent men around 'after the revolution' is too late, and we know from revolutionary history that change may not extend past the front door. In newly socialised countries such as Nicaragua there is some recognition, in work in countering machismo, of the tenacity of possessive and therefore oppressive intimacy.

As women found to their cost, cohabitation can be just as oppressive as its legal parent if the same possessiveness applies. It is not merely that men get to possess women. A woman's feeling of possessiveness of her male partner is part of an effective dependency and the relationship becomes all-important, regardless of the quality of it or its destructive powers. There has always been a cynical acknowledgement of this in common-sense understanding, yet the strength of the idea of the couple and the family has overcome any unease about the potential negative consequences. Although it is increasingly less true in reality, social mythology clings to the idea that women need men for financial and physical security, and that to be without a man is to be without life:

> Ridiculed by men, treated with scornful anxiety by other women, the old maid is a traditional figure of fun. Men without women may achieve a certain romantic panache; women without men are oddities, hardly women at all.
>
> (Gissing, 1980, Introduction)

Given the driving (but assumed) need to be part of a couple, it is not surprising that the period of time spent getting to know someone well enough to declare a relationship produces its own set of situations and ideas which can allow rape to occur. The problem with courtship as a relationship is its ambivalence. Separated into two spheres, and having developed views of the world and even languages which differ, in courtship female and male are thrown together and expected to understand each other. Thanks to cynicism, they usually do. However, courtship assumes a form of equality where the separate roles, needs and explanations will be negotiated fairly. Because it is connected with intimacy, there is also an assumption of trust that the point of the relationship is the mutual enjoyment and well-being of both. It is possible, but these unwritten rules can also be broken.

In order for intentional victimisation to occur, the victimiser has to be able to find and use an opportunity, first to make the intended victim vulnerable and then to commit the victimising act. In the case of rape, the courtship situation provides a number of ways for a man to create the right conditions for victimisation. To begin with, the fact of knowing someone takes a woman's mind completely away from common-sense understandings of the dangers from rape. The rapist is not, according to theory, the guy next door, a boyfriend, a friend's boyfriend, brother or brother's friend, plumber, postman, etc. Some of these social roles are clearly defined as non-sexual, others (as with dating) are ambivalent about sexual content but 'clearly' violence is not a risk. The trust that the rules we live by will be adhered to by all is necessary for social existence. That trust both helps us to live in relative safety (because most people do abide by the rules) and helps to mask the intentions of the few who mean us harm. Abusing trust may then be the first step in victimisation through rape.

Once involved in a relationship, whatever its basis or intensity, it can usually be assumed that those involved will respond to each other as people and not as role models, and that each other's needs will be taken into account. There are two interfering components of the feminine/masculine divide which hinder this. Firstly, women will be expected to defer to men and will be assumed to be doing so even when they are not. For example, in conversation, women will often act as feeds to men who will lead the conversation. If a woman attempts to change the conversation, her contribution may well be ignored. This means that, if there is a difference between what a man wants from a meeting and what a woman wants, his intention has the better chance of being seen through. Secondly, the passive feminine characteristics do not provide women with sufficient self-will to assert their own needs and intentions. 'Niceness' is a passive quality in women much appreciated. Quiet, unassuming, never making waves or causing a scene. A man who intends harm can use this niceness to first hide his intentions, then to prevent a woman making her concern explicit when she has begun to see her true situation. Women who have struggled and stopped a sexual encounter firmly have been met with the words, 'OK, don't panic. I didn't mean anything. I won't rape you, you know.' Such a response trivialises a woman's concern and blames her for over-reaction. In effect, if a man intends harm to a woman, he can use both the dominance in masculinity and the subservience in femininity to manipulate a situation.

Intimacy contains vulnerability to rape because of the opportunity in a private and exclusive relationship for abuse and because the basis of the relationship itself contains the potential for victimisation. Courtship adds the confusion of ambivalence, where victimisation can be hidden and covered up with excuses. Feminism, in exposing these problems, was not arguing for an end to intimacy and true relationships, but for an end to the inequalities that the current structure imposes on personal lives. Take away the benefits of intimacy, and look at how male and female interact as relative strangers, and the problems become even clearer.

The problem for women dealing with men in non-intimate situations is that there is no model to measure behaviour against, except that women should tread a tightrope between being pleasant and remaining suitably distant. One of the double binds of rape is that a woman who accepts male company at face value could remain with her assumptions of trust, and her motives for being with him, intact – unless he chooses to rape her. In that case, her motive in being with him is assumed to be provocative, or may at least be questioned. If the only images of women we have are those of mother or whore, then there is no understanding of women as workmates, friends or just other people in the street. Once out of the 'safe' surroundings of home and family, the world could become problematic.

In the beginning of the 'new wave', feminism concentrated on the limited job opportunities for women, either in the professions or as equal workers in terms of pay and conditions. Once at work (and, contrary to the myth, women did and always have been a significant part of the economic world), the experience of workers as *women* showed that the problems of women's oppression had only just begun:

> Disapproval of sexual harassment tends to focus on demands for sex as a condition of hiring as well as for keeping a job. These are considered serious manifestations of sexual coercion, while generalised staring, commenting, touching, and other forms of male familiarity are regarded as annoying and of little consequence. The outright demand for sex appears more serious because the economic penalties for noncompliance are easily discernible and the consequences to both the woman who refuses and the woman who submits against her will are easily imagined. Sexual harassment is nevertheless an act of aggression at any stage of its expression, and in all its forms it contributes to the ultimate goal of keeping women subordinate at work.
>
> (Farley, 1978, p. 15)

Predictably, the popular press and other conservative minds trivialised the situation and the feminist concern. The male conservatives had become too used to decorating work space with female bodies, of having women around for their own pleasure, while like-minded women were used to finding status in being treated as pin-ups and blow-up dolls. The system which saw servants as things, not people, was reproduced in the workplace where women (in the main) take up the subordinate, servicing roles. The lower status combined with being female is another situation for potential victimisation. This time it could be denied altogether, by saying that women either enjoyed it or at least didn't mind men's 'bit of fun'. Those who did notice, and did mind sexual harassment, found a voice in feminism for their own views, rather than the views of those with a vested interest in silencing the complaints of the abused workers.

Travelling between work and home, or any other need to be in the streets, faced women with another relationship with men – as strangers. When faced with male familiarity or downright abuse in the streets, the almost universal response is to walk on, head down, pretending not to have noticed. A few women say they enjoy the attention, others that it is a mild embarrassment, while others find the intrusion into their private space annoying. The issue is whether men regard women as public property or private individuals. Men have answered that the intention is only to be friendly, but why then is there often a sexual connotation and why don't men say hello to other men? Men rarely mention the very explicit or threatening comments women have to endure. The overall effect, whatever they say, is to deny women the right to personal space in public and to demand women's attention whether they want it or not.

Feminism was not totally devoid of smart answers back – the displayed genitalia and proud question 'what do you think this is baby!' can be met with 'it looks like a penis – only smaller' (feminist legend). In the early days, women took to hanging around on street corners whistling at men, which was a (half) joking answer back to the 'friendly' male attention; it also proved to be a major irritant to the male targets. It was, at least, an active response. Whether embarrassed or angry, a lowered head and passive reaction cannot have any effect at all.

An early feminist study of sexual violence, *Against Rape*, (Medea and Thompson, 1974) called sexual harassment at work and on the streets 'little rapes'. This made the connection between the overall situation of women, the background of abuse we live with, and the actual violence of rape and sexual assault. There are other manifestations of violence, personal and political, which added to the feminist belief that rape itself is not an aberration, but that society itself is somewhat odd.

FACING THE BULLY – THE PROBLEM WITH MALE VIOLENCE

Feminism did not have to look directly at rape to see the vicious effects of masculine stereotyping. New Wave Feminism grew up surrounded by the 'peace' following World War II. 'Peace' as shown in Korea, the Middle East, Ireland, South Africa, Vietnam, Bangladesh, Hungary, and, of course, the 'cold' war – the relationship between the USSR and the US which closely resembled the aggressive posturing of two overblown male egos. The revolutionary alternatives of the 1960s and 1970s were spoken of in the same language of violence and male aggression. Feminism has always seen the connection between the political structure, the situation of women, and personal experiences. Equally, political aggression and individual male behaviour feeds one into the other.

At the heart of militarism and political aggression lies fear. In a world which is organised around principles of inequality, competition, patriotism, and greed, the key organisers and workers need suitable personal qualities, i.e. the self-concern, aggression and ambition of the masculine model. When it suits the political system, such attributes are well rewarded and such positions jealously guarded. Capitalists fear socialism for the same reason men may not want to see women's equality, because they believe that it will mean less for them, as well it might.

There is another, more basic, fear too. The arms race is a clear example of 'my dad's bigger than your dad' political thinking. Fear of the misuse of superior strengths fires the guns of war, and the tempers in street brawls. It is the reason why inequality is both enduring and fragile. In the case of gender, the fallback justification for inequality is the 'natural' superior strengths of men over women leading, apparently, to them becoming therefore 'natural' leaders. There was, in the mists of time, a reasonably logical explanation for a discrepancy or distribution of strengths between the sexes. The protection of children and the relatively long period of immaturity for humans would have influenced the physical size and strength of men as a social protection for the immature while women's greater endurance would have helped with the drains on strength of the mothering role and pregnancy. While this was important in the early development of humans, and may even still play a part in societies where physical attributes are necessary for survival, it is nothing more than an evolutionary hang-up in this society:

The value placed on physical strength which reinforced the dominance of men, and the male superiority attitudes that this generated,
have also become dysfunctional. It is the mind, not the body, which
must now prevail, and woman's mind is the equal of man's.

(Freeman, 1970, p. 15)

Life is cheerfully described in jungle terms by the pinstriped
Tarzans of the financial centres of the world, as if there still
existed for them a real and clear relationship between their own
survival and a hostile nature, but it is fanciful. Equally, the
importance put on physical differences to explain away civil or
social inequality would be laughable except that the conditions
such attitudes create are not so funny for many women. The
heavy male may now be dysfunctional, but he survives and is
encouraged in his out-of-date conceit. The encouragement is not
only towards feeling superior, however unrealistic in the individual case, but also towards proving the difference. One way
of showing off is rape.

The supposition of superior strength is certainly one factor
which allows rape to occur, for without a difference being at
least believed to exist, rape would not be a possibility as an act
aimed by men at women. In order for intentional victimisation
to be practised, according to victimology, there has to be a
discrepancy of strength or a weakness which can be used:

The weak specimen, in the animal kingdom and in mankind, is the
most likely to be the victim of an attack.

(von Hentig 1948, p. 404)*

The discrepancy in strength may not have to exist in reality as
long as it is believed to exist. The belief in superior male
strength both emboldens men and weakens women, so when
tested in practice, as in rape, the belief itself acts as effectively
as weight-training versus shrivelled muscles would.

For such discrepancy to be taken advantage of, there has to be
another factor which is often left out in classic victimology or
other discussions of the role of the victim in the commission of
crimes. The feminist search for an understanding of rape
started with normal, everyday life and so saw that discrepancies
and differences exist all around without necessarily causing

* I have not questioned or highlighted the use of 'kingdom' or 'mankind' here to
describe groups which are patently not male only. This quote refers, it seems,
specifically to male behaviour, so may as well be left as a sexist reference.

hardship or pain. Children are necessarily weak and dependent, but millions grow up without suffering at the hands of those bigger and older. Children also are caught up in victimisation, however, if the potential victimiser *chooses* to use the perceived weakness or vulnerability to create victimisation. The fundamental root of victimisation through rape, therefore, is the willingness of some men to commit it and the associated willingness of society to condone their actions. Within this society, there is no automatic revulsion at acts which oppress the weak or disadvantaged; in fact it is taken as normal and, if the victimiser gains as a result, as laudable efforts at working the system. The prehistoric mentality prevails with 'to the victor the spoils' and holds us all back from reaching a system more suitable for our times.

The raw picture painted here will be rejected or criticised as outrageous by those who have a vested interest in maintaining the status quo – which means maintaining rape. They will want rape to be considered as a deviant act. Yet, work which has looked at the 'real' rapists (the ones caught out) actually backs up the view that there is a close similarity between accepted and valued masculinity and the attributes necessary to commit rape.

In the attempt to set apart those whom society deems to be deviant, the search goes on for a particular 'criminal type' – eyes too close together, sticky-out ears and head-bumps have all been seriously considered to show a criminal nature in the past. A recurrent idea is that such 'types' are regressive throwbacks to a less civilised human form. (Interestingly, the corresponding research on female deviance suggests the problem for women is a regression to male characteristics.) The search for the true rapist has gone on within this wider debate. Any understanding of rape assumes that sex and aggression are necessary components. In looking for an abnormality in rapists, the search has concentrated on looking then at abnormal sexual or aggressive behaviour or attitudes.

Considering, first, aggression, whether biologically or culturally grounded, there is no denying that in some circumstances it is seen as valuable – in men. As with sex, aggression is often seen as a drive or force which can get out of hand, but not as a factor which never plays a useful part. If translated into such terms as dominance and assertiveness, aggression is associated with normal male sexuality, even, but erroneously, as part of male attractiveness to women. The assumption is often that rapists will be 'too' aggressive or out of control of their aggression. Studies, however, do not give a clear answer. Some will indicate that some rapists are prone towards highly aggressive behaviour, or aggression only in some situations and with specific stimulation (e.g. some rapists are only aggressive with women). Other studies show that rapists can also be non-aggressive or measured as weak and ineffectual compared with the general ideals of masculinity. Just like other men then, rapists can be seen as either studs or wimps, but most will be somewhere between the two.

When sex is considered as a component of rape, then neither an overwhelming sexual need or a need for abnormal sexual practices is a necessary component of rape. In fact, sexual dysfunction (measured by lack of an erection or ejaculation) is not an uncommon factor and, whatever acts are committed during rape, they can often be taken as normal enough if they occur within mutually pleasing love-making. The deviance of rape seems to lie with a man's ability to have sex with someone he knows does not want it. Since it is part of social mythology that women will have sex when they don't want to, even the will of a raped woman does not separate rape from other sexual acts, in general thinking. (It is, of course, the key difference in feminist thought.)

When sexuality is broadened to include other related personality traits, or if the roots of a rapist's sexuality are investigated, factors begin to emerge which can be related to behaviour. For example, studies of rapists have indicated that some have a negative assessment of women, particularly in a sexual context. Others find it difficult to form affectionate relationships. One study summed its findings up thus:

> ... what there is in common [among sex offenders] is ... an absence of mature, selfless concern for the victim of his obsession, an inability to live in a desexualised manner, a terrible sadness and sense of loneliness, a lack of sublimation, and a totally narcissistic, self-centred orientation.
>
> (Cohen and Bouchier, 1972, p. 62)

It may be a question of degree, but neither a dislike nor contempt for women, nor suppression of male emotional expression, nor a self-centred orientation is lacking in normal

male socialisation and in the masculine model. In total, there is
nothing inherently deviant, in the context of this society, about
either aggression or sex, or for that matter a combination of the
two.

The difference between a portrait of glorious machismo and
the sketch here of the thoroughly normal rapist is a difference in
viewpoint only, but viewpoint can mean everything. Where the
Old Colonials saw death, glory and the Empire, feminism looked through the eyes of those outside the system and saw death
certainly, but vanity and the theft of land and livelihood from
those who could not or did not protect themselves. Where pinstriped apes see character and the right spirit, feminism sees
aggression, self-centredness and potential brutality. A husband
who has beaten his wife may be regarded by some others as a
real man showing true authority, but the eyes of his wife see
only a bully. Society still sees a sexually exciting image when
presented with the viewpoint of the rapist by a trash press. Rape
is not thrilling, and the victim is not distant and safely in the
realms of myth. It is violent, and she is right here and she is
everyone's problem.

The rape which feminism is concerned about bears little
resemblance to the rape studied by psychologists and understood by the rest of this society. Feminism rejected the model of
the lone deviant, acting out perverted fantasies or frustrations,
and substituted instead a figure who had an uncomfortable
similarity to the average man. It also rejected the 'overpowering
urge' (or should that be 'lame excuse'), and called the reason
men rape, their choice.

In changing the viewpoint, we also rejected the trivialisation
of rape as rough love-making or the complaints of a jilted ex-
lover. Instead, the focus of attention was on what victimisation
actually entailed for women who had been raped. With an
emphasis on understanding rape as part of women's lives, what
was uncovered was the process of victimisation and what it
could mean.

ANOTHER FORM OF VIOLENCE – RAPE AND RACE

'New Wave' feminism grew up in the years when the 'melting
pot' view of race relations predominated. Full unity would be

achieved if only we could all forget our differences and integrate. It is a comfortable philosophy for white liberals. What it could mean for the ethnic minorities in white, western societies is the loss of their own heritage. It is perhaps no coincidence that the 'melting pot' grew alongside Black Power and other manifestations of cultural consciousness which protected uniqueness. As a counter, white racism and apartheid in its many forms show that a personal disowning of a colonial history is not enough to end oppression through race. Similar patterns could be seen in the Women's Liberation Movements, with the fight for equality and integration into the system balanced by a rise in a separatist movement, and the focus on a unique women's history and culture. There is even a reactionary right wing women's movement.

When feminism met the 'melting pot', there was a tendency for white liberal feminists to believe that we were all one, and that differences in colour were not relevant to feminism. In a similar vein, the focus on sexuality as the key issue left many working-class and black women feeling that their own experiences of oppression were being ignored or trivialised in favour of a preoccupation of middle-class, white women. Alison Edwards (1976), writing for the Sojourner Truth Organisation, commented on Susan Brownmiller's book, *Against Our Will*, that the feminist analysis of rape assumed that black women factory workers would have more in common with Happy Rockefeller than their black male co-workers. Clearly, an analysis of oppression which could not take in the effects of race, class and other forms of inequality, was going to remain limited. The lesson was that being female, just like being black, was not a political statement itself; the politics came with what we decided to do about it.

There have been problems with the continuing view that all that is needed is for all women to come together, for not only has the situation for black and Asian women been misunderstood, but the role of right-wing women in attacking feminism also is lost. As far as rape is concerned, taking race into account both shows the validity of some of the feminist understanding, and exposes issues around rape which have not been fully acknowledged.

The process of victimisation through rape involves the polarisation of the genders into opposing stereotypes which are

limiting and oppressive in themselves. A similar process has
created racist stereotypes of the minority groups in Western
society. The most commonly understood must be the images
created from the white racist view of slavery – the black
'mammy' as the Good Woman and her counterpart in an
animalistic view of young black women's rampant sexuality.
These are gross exaggerations of all female role models.
Similarly, we end up with the meek and obedient Asian wife and
the black male stud. They are white male fantasies, fed back to
us all. These images fuel the way we view rape, and influence
society's handling of victimisation. For example, inter-racial
rape is not common. As women are more likely to be raped by
men known to them, so those men are likely to be of the same
colour. Yet the fear of other races is strong, and the white male
fear of the sexual strength of black maleness adds to this fear of
differentness for white women. For black women, the fear of
whites is added to by the knowledge that white men have both
fantasies of black sexuality, and a history of racial sexual abuse
behind them. Although the research is unclear, anecdotal
evidence would suggest that white women reporting black
stranger-rapists are more likely to be believed than black
women reporting whites. For many women (black or white)
raped by black men, the knowledge that their colour not their
actions would count against them, as far as the police are
concerned, is a consideration when deciding whether to make
their experience a 'crime'.

There are parallels between the relevance of race to rape with
rape in wartime. In political conflict, rape is committed by the
victorious troops against women on the defeated side, or as a
considered act of aggression during the progress of the fighting.
Either way, rape is designed to humiliate and degrade the
opposition – the opposing men, that is, for the attack is on male
property. Rape in this situation is also an expression of contempt. How similar are the sexual assaults by the police on
women demonstrators or political prisoners, and by racist gangs
and the security forces of countries such as South Africa on
black and Asian women? The rape of white women is also one
way for white men to be attacked, and the comment of Eldridge
Cleaver that he saw the rape of white women as a political act,
hurt women in the Women's Movement in the 1960s and was
part of the conflict between the 'white' Women's Movement and

male radicals in the US. We have all learned more about the 'connectedness' of oppression, including Eldridge Cleaver, and can see more clearly that, whatever the reason for rape and whoever is the primary target, women get hurt.

There are times, though, when rape is used directly to criminalise and victimise black and Asian men, as South Africa now, and the southern US states in the past, have indicated most clearly. Whether there has been a true relationship between a woman and a man or not, if the state or community decides that mixed-race sexual relations are wrong, or that the accusation of rape is a useful weapon against an ethnic or cultural group, then false claims of rape have been made, and not necessarily by the woman concerned. Such claims may result from actual rape, or may be a right-wing woman's contribution to black victimisation. Whatever the truth in any particular case, the false claims serve both to achieve the aim of racist harassment, and trivialise the actual victimisation of women.

Rape, taken in the context of race, can be viewed in two ways. Either rape as a crime against all women is the central concern, where race is used as one way of defining the target of victimisation, or rape is used in a racist attack, because women are vulnerable and because sexual violence is a specific and effective form of humiliation or expression of contempt. What is clear is that racism has its own process of victimisation imposed on the non-dominant cultures in society, and reflected in people's individual lives.

RAPE AS A PROCESS OF VICTIMISATION

The understanding of rape outlined so far locates the start of the process of victimisation at birth or before. Here, rape can be seen as a product of the unequal power relations existing between the sexes, written into the codes of conduct passed on to us as masculine and feminine models. After looking at rape, masculine and feminine seem more like rules for classic victimiser/ victimised roles than guides for comfortable living. In short, by encouraging male superiority and constantly belittling the female in society, it becomes possible for men to abuse their position of power by oppressing women. This can explain how rape can occur, but does not answer the question of why. The political or social situation of women is a factor in creating the vulnerability which is necessary before victimisation can occur, but it does not create rape itself.

Feminism raised the hackles of many men, whether sympathetic to the cause or not, by saying in the early days of the campaign against rape that all men are potential rapists. To the extent that all men are socialised towards an aggressive masculinity and encouraged to see women as inferior to themselves, then the statement is true. What changes potential to actual is the individual man's decision to become a rapist, backed by society's ambivalent attitude towards that choice. The debates around the relative weaknesses of women and our vulnerability can fall into the trap of assuming that femininity plays some part in causing rape. What causes rape is man's choice – to perpetuate inequality and to commit an individual act. In looking at the process of victimisation, two further questions of why and how are addressed – why men choose rape and how it is achieved.

In order for an act of intentional victimisation to be committed, it is necessary for some reason or motive to occur or be chosen by the victimiser. Instead of the commonly understood reason of 'I couldn't help myself' or some other overwhelming urge, feminism saw clearly that the basic reason men had for raping women was contempt. Susan Griffin, in an article which had an important influence at the start of the feminist debate, saw the connection between the contempt shown in rape and the inherent conflict in feminine and masculine models:

> For in our culture, heterosexual love finds an erotic expression through male dominance and female submission. A man who derives pleasure from raping a woman must enjoy force and dominance as much as or more than the simple pleasures of the flesh ... and if the professional rapist is to be separated from the average dominant heterosexual, it may be mainly a quantitative difference.
> (Griffin, 1971, p. 3)

Passive femininity is seen as being translated from the ideal model into real situations where women are unable to exert their will or defend themselves if necessary and where masculinity can be translated into overwhelming dominance. In effect, what was being described was rape as a logical conclusion of normal interaction, in this society at least.

If male contempt for feminine women can be seen to be one

way that the feminine/masculine separation is translated into rape, equally male anger at women who do not toe the feminine line comes up as a reason for rape:

> In particular, it appears that rape is a punitive action directed towards females who usurp or appear to usurp the culturally defined prerogatives of the dominant male role ... it appeared that the girls were behaving in ways that violated the traditional double standards of sexual morality but were applying a rigorous standard of their own in selecting and rejecting sexual partners. The fact that they did so with glee added insult to injury from the males' perspective.
>
> (Reynolds, 1972, p. 67)

It would seem a no-win situation when women can be raped for behaving as society asks them to, because by doing so they are defenceless against those men who would abuse their position, and raped for breaking out of the feminine mould, because that challenges male power and threatens the status quo. Whether it is a man who has decided that he will get what he wants regardless and chooses his moment, or one who feels he has been slighted by a woman and decides on revenge, or just one who needs to put someone into an inferior position to himself and finds his target in a woman, it is possible to see that social contempt for women can be translated into personal victimisation.

Rather than sexual satisfaction as a motive for rape, which has been the social understanding, women who had been raped presented sexual humiliation as the more obvious desire of the rapists. If the question why is asked, as in 'why sexual violence', then it can be seen that as a weapon which acts through humiliation, rape is highly effective. Sex is clearly connected in this society with dominance and power. By using a parody of an intimate act, rape gets through to the core of the woman it is used against. In committing rape, the individual rapist can be expressing feelings of ownership, hatred, power and revenge. In not dealing with rape appropriately, society is dealing with women in much the same way.

Although not starting now with birth and the social situation of women, the process around any individual act of victimisation through rape still starts before the act itself. The common misunderstanding about rape has always been that it is an explosive act, taking over and erupting outside the control of the rapist. A major study of rape was published by Menachim Amir

(1971). The study was of police records of rape and looked, possibly for the first time in such a systematic way, at the events leading up to rape. Amir concluded that a majority of rapes contain some degree of premeditation or planning on the part of the rapist. This was taken up by feminists as a missing part of the jigsaw, for in acknowledging the taking of control and clear decision-making, the translation from socialisation into personal action was made. The planning contains many of the elements necessary to victimise another – the using or creating of opportunities to get a woman alone, thereby increasing her vulnerability, and manipulating social situations to effectively psychologically disarm her.

In another concept, of victim precipitation, Amir also outlined the necessary justifications that the offender would make as reasons for the victimisation: blaming the woman for behaviour which was unfeminine (and therefore put her outside the bounds of male protection); claiming that it was not rape because she had encouraged a sexual act; she deserved punishment for some slight against the rapist; she had given up the right to decide for herself about sex because of previous sexual activity. Although called victim precipitation, implying that the woman concerned knew what was to happen and encouraged it, these explanations were 'techniques of neutralisation' (first discussed in terms of delinquency by Sykes and Matza, 1957). They were useful ways of understanding the excuses that a rapist will offer, and may even have convinced himself of, but not explanations of female behaviour or responsibility. From the woman's point of view, which is ignorant of the rapist's intentions, she is doing nothing provocative. In truth, the only provocation the rapists are acknowledging is that the woman was female and existed – it is all that they needed to know.

During the act itself, although the woman can sense the rapist's motives or experiences, the meaning of rape is not about dominance, but about being out of control or totally under the control of another. One early study of women's reactions to rape, by Burgess and Holmstrom (1975), described rape as a 'life-threatening' situation when women felt that, in a very real sense, they faced death by losing control over their lives. An understanding of this experience became a major part of the feminist response to raped women, as counselling and other support services were built up around the idea of allowing a woman to regain the control that had been taken away. It was an important step also away from the idea of the passive victim.

In the end, what feminists confronted in changing views on rape was society's understanding of victimisation. The idea of a 'victim' in this competitive, unequal and cruel society carries with it connotations of being the loser, now and for always. We have no time for anyone other than the winners, and it can be part of the rules of the game that someone is hurt. Being a 'victim' is a passive state to be in, and feels like a description of an object. In total, society is made uncomfortable by victims, and can only cope by being kind to them (if they are weak and vulnerable enough to warrant sympathy), or by denying that they exist. When women confronted rape, the denial was also confronted. Society's sympathy was hardly any improvement, given that the patronising and controlling offices of the do-gooders would expect passive victims lining up for their benefits. The experience of rape, from the social undercurrents through to the act itself, showed to women the dangers that can lie in becoming dependent on others, which welfare largesse implies. What was needed was the space to deal with victimisation on women's own terms and under our own control.

The final part of the process, then, becomes not an adjustment to being a victim but an active reassessment of the world and a learning to understand and assimilate an experience into life. The point of looking at the whole process of victimisation is to see not only the rape, but women overcoming it.

2 RESEARCHING RAPE

Hopefully, it will not sound too pompous to say that we believed the research to be important beyond this time and place or we could not have done it.

(Holmes and Williams, 1978, p. 14)

There were three major influences on the development of this study of women's experiences of rape. The first was the fact that I was a member of the collective which started the London Rape Crisis Centre, and so needed information for myself. The second was a background in sociology and an interest in research, and the third was a specific interest in seeing a feminist influence on social theory and practice worked out. My active involvement in the Anti-Rape Campaign defined for me the kind of research I wanted to see done, and a feminist understanding helped to focus how it could be done. A sociological background let me know what was around and all three influences combined in convincing me to do the research for myself. There was, when I started, very little work that was really of use in providing information about what rape meant to women, but that is not true now. The last decade has seen a positive and wide ranging increase in interest in rape as a subject, in the effects on women, and what could be done to change the situation.

RAPE AS THE SUBJECT OF RESEARCH

The changes in our understanding of rape reflect changes in beliefs about women, inequality, and criminal behaviour, as well as changes in legal and social practices. For example, while the concern of the law was to test out a woman's account, believing that most allegations of rape were false, then the literature would also focus on the unproven and why women made 'false' claims of rape (possibly based on the woman's withdrawal of the complaint; we do now understand a little better what pressures may be behind such a move). The image of the women who had suffered rape was, before the 1970s, quite unclear. If the predominant view was that rape was the result of individual aberration and uncontrollable sexual urges, then the woman victimised was to some extent irrelevant because the choice of her as a 'victim' would be unconnected with her as an individual – purely accidental. Only within victimology, where the relationship between the offender and offended is the main concern, would personal characteristics matter, and then only those defined as such by the rapist or the researcher.

The real forerunner of rape research which focused on those victimised by it, was the work of the patronising, scandalised do-gooding social commentators of the turn of the century. The concern for the impoverished, or those lost to lust, actually focused more on child prostitution and the abuse of the young than on the rape of adult women, but the attitudes were the same. The answers for them came not in changing the system, but in changing the 'victims' – removing young women from the demoralising effects of poverty, by Good Works.

Early radical feminist writing also addressed the issue of prostitution and the sexual abuse of women. The problem was not seen as just the warping effects of dirt and poverty, but primarily as the position of women at the very bottom of the pile. Wealth did not make women safe from all harassment and victimisation, but work and rights which would ensure real equality would. Again, the issue of rape was not the obvious subject, but as a historical background to the feminism of the 1960s and 1970s, the thinking and experiences behind the work of women such as Emma Goldman, Stella Brown and Alexandra Kollontai (Kollontai, 1972) becomes important.

One fundamental reason why the feminist anti-rape campaigns created such a change in thinking about rape was that they gave space and voice to those who had been silenced. Instead of the offender, the offended were able to put their side of the story. The development of support services meant that women who had been raped became more visible, through their own choice. Information was often collected as part of support giving, and this information was radically different from that contained by the police and clinical records previously relied on.

In the decade and a half since the first Rape Crisis Centres set up in the US, rape has been looked at from a myriad aspects, some following on from classic and radical past views, and others applying new perspectives. It is worth a review of the areas research has moved into because all, in diversity, offer something toward an understanding of women's experiences.

Those who rape

The main question behind the study of rapists is usually 'why do they do it?' Whether the approach assumes a psychological problem which takes choice away from the individual rapist, or takes into account conscious decision-making, some form of profile based on motive or personality type usually results. Cohen *et al.* 1971 published studies defining psychological profiles of rapists which analysed the individual's background and act in terms of sexual or aggressive motivations. Their categories of 'sexual', 'aggressive' and 'aggressive-sexual' have been used, tested and adapted frequently since then. Their work also helped to shift the focus of attention from rape as a purely sexual act to an understanding of the violence involved.

Other researchers, rather than look at the rapists' backgrounds as a whole, have chosen instead to analyse specific possible influences on behaviour which could 'push' a man towards the act of rape. A wide variety of factors have been looked at including a man's relationship with his father or mother, violence in the childhood home environment, sexual fantasies, attitudes towards homosexuality and attitudes towards women. Some general points have emerged, for example, that rapists can see themselves as macho men, or weak and wimpy; that some hold extremely pure images of women (so find most women unworthy) and some think of all women as dirty and contemptible; or that some will use any opportunity which arises (such as burglary) to rape, others plan and organise the attack, and some seek out a target when the mood takes them (Brodsky *et al.* 1977; Scott and Tetreault, 1987). Taken as a whole, the studies show us only the diversity of rapists.

The first widely read criminological study of rape as a recorded crime was Amir's (1971). His and later work which refined the approach, such as *Patterns of Rape in England* (Wright, 1980) related an individual's commission of the crime of rape to the social situation he was in. The intention was to view the rapist as a criminal and to understand further the reasoning behind and commission of a criminal offence. Lorrenne Clark and Debra Lewis (1977), studying police records in Canada, analysed both the record collecting and the results in terms of more general social attitudes to rape and to women.

Studies of men who have not been recorded as rapists (whether because they are men who have chosen not to rape or because they are men who have the same attributes and attitudes but have not been 'labelled' criminal) could provide valuable insight into why rape happens. This has not yet really developed as an area, but close to this type of work are the studies of male sexual aggression in what would be considered 'normal' situations. The first study of this kind, by Kirkpatrick and Kanin (1957) was published well before the influence of the Women's Movement but in some ways tested its ideas. The study looked at dating relationships among students and the reports of sexual aggression given by both men and women. This, and the studies which have followed, have indicated that aggressive behaviour in order to force sexual activity on women is more widespread than the figures for rape alone; that in some ways the relationship between men and women contains the potential for violence and conflict.

Work on both physical violence only, and on rape has looked within marriage. This is still not considered a crime in most countries or states and so it remains one platform of the political anti-rape campaign. Diana Russell, who has worked on rape research from the beginning of the 1970s, published in 1982 her study of rape in marriage. Of 644 married women interviewed, eighty-seven disclosed at least one incidence of rape or attempted rape, or about 14 per cent. This is an uncomfortable statistic which does not in itself show a universal conflict between female and male, but begins to locate rape within the core of our society.

Those who are raped

When the focus of attention turned to the women who had experienced rape, the concern was with finding out about the effects of rape, the better to counteract them.

One of the first reports on rape produced from a feminist perspective was a self-report survey based on a questionnaire published in a popular women's magazine, and as the book *Against Rape* (Medea and Thompson, 1974). The study suffered from the problems inherent in self-report work, that the women who responded may not be 'representative' of all raped women, compounded by the obvious bias produced by the limits of the magazine readership. However, the search for the perfect sample can detract from using the information we can get and have got, and *Against Rape* provided some useful insights into the range of experiences women included under the label 'rape' as well as the variety of feelings and responses such experiences produced. Most of the research on women's experiences has, as this early work did, gone beyond the official statistics and tried to reach into the 'unreported' area of rape, an area almost everyone involved would now acknowledge as including far more victimisation than the rate of reported rape ever does.

The studies coming from the new and developing services can be divided into three overall types. The first are those which looked at women's reactions to rape, in a sense cataloguing the extent and variations. Second are those which concentrate on a specific set of reactions in order to understand more fully where those reactions come from and how they fit into women's overall response. Third are those which look at response as a wide process, involving a complex web of reactions and a specific pattern over time. In their book, *Understanding the Rape Victim*, Sedelle Katz and Mary Ann Mazur (1979) provided a comprehensive review of the literature on women's personal responses to rape, comparing findings across studies wherever possible and taking into account the problems created by different methods. Although not intended to do this, the survey of studies was an early indication of the connection between the sexual assault of adult women, and of children.

As well as looking at overall responses, research has looked at specific areas of women's lives and the effect of rape. Studies focused on sexuality or sexual responses, personal or emotional recovery, relationships, and how a woman's social life or work situation could be affected. Beverley Atkeson's work on depression (1982) Patricia Resick on Social Adjustment (1981 [161]) and Dean Kilpatrick's (1981) analysis of the 'fear response' in women who have been raped, are good examples of the range of work which has gone on.

An early paper called 'Patterns of response among victims

of rape', (Sutherland and Scherl, 1970) outlined a three-stage pattern of response over time, which many studies since have either used as a base or tested in their own work. Burgess and Holmstrom (1975, 1978), throughout their long-term research begun in the early 1970s, also worked around a pattern or 'syndrome' effect, similar to the Sutherland and Scherl model but primarily noting two stages. This type of work was particularly useful to those giving support to raped women, as it helped our understanding of the changing effect of the experience as it went into a woman's past rather than present.

The other aspects of rape

If the work with men shows us how many reasons a man may have for committing rape, and if the work with raped women shows us the diversity of women's responses, then an overview of the literature shows us equally the variety of ways in which the social impact of rape can be viewed.

The law. Since the early 1970s, work on the law on rape has increased dramatically and also changed in focus. A decade ago, the main focus of legal discussions was on the treatment of women by the law and legal process, and the remedies possible which would give women a fairer hearing when defining their experience as a crime. This discussion could take place either in work specifically related to rape, or within the wider perspective of the sexism inherent in the legal practice and theory. In work collected together in one special volume of a journal, for example Babcock (1973) looking at women and the criminal justice system, a clear idea can be gained of the range of issues and how rape fits into more general political and ideological debate. By now the legal concerns have shifted slightly, so that changes in the law or procedure which have taken place in the last ten years are being critically overhauled to see if they have in fact produced the desired effects – to improve the reporting rates and develop a legal system in which all women feel they can seek security and redress.

Rape as social control. At the very beginning of the feminist concern with rape, the idea that rape was a form of social control on women was widely discussed and formed a rallying cry for the Anti-Rape Campaign. In fact, it was argued that the *fear*, as well as the experience, of rape was the social control, for fear keeps women isolated, looking for protection and looking to stay out of the way. An interesting focus of research has been the testing of the idea that fear is a form of social control, either looking specifically at women's fear of rape, or as part of a wider view of the role of fear in victimisation. Studies have so far tended to indicate that the fear of rape is greater than the actual incidence would warrant, and that to some extent women keep within boundaries they feel safe in (though whether this is the fear of rape specifically, or a more general feeling of vulnerability as women, is still being debated).

An interesting progression has been research into actual and felt vulnerability to assault (Burt and Katz, 1975). The increased awareness of rape, necessary if rape was to be taken seriously, could have contributed to a greater fear, or women could assume it was something that happened to someone else, their task being only to avoid being the type of woman who was raped. Taking blame away from the 'victim' also meant increasing an awareness of vulnerability, whatever 'type' of woman you were. Sensationalisation of crime gives women and the elderly the impression that they are particularly vulnerable to violent crime; it is this which has inspired the studies which assess real vulnerability, assumed vulnerability and suggestions of how to make those unsettled feel more secure and less restricted.

In the field of victimology generally, there are developments which are relevant to an understanding of rape. One area is the analysis of how people make the choice of whether to call their victimisation a crime or not (Feldman-Summers and Ashworth, 1981). Also, the relationship between the 'victim' and the offender has been a constant theme, the main theme really, of victimology. Here perhaps is where rape research has had a wider influence, in that it has helped to clarify the definition of 'victim' and the distinction between blame, responsibility, precipitation and participation.

Within feminist concerns, the issue of pornography has developed alongside that of rape. A decade ago, all criticism of pornography seemed to be silenced by the liberal defenders of 'free speech' by associating feminism with right-wing repression. Studies have seriously explored the connection between public images such as pornography and sexual violence, any clear results being blurred by the complexity of the relationship. A clearer basis for discussion has developed, however, for now the issue is not that pornography causes sexual violence but that it is in itself a form of violence and needs to be studied and reacted to as such.

One problem with research into rape is that we are not yet able to really talk about long-term effects with certainty, with studies which have followed women for periods of more than a couple of years. This may in fact prove a burden too heavy to ask women to carry – after all, the point of research would be to help reduce the time that women felt they were 'victims' and not to prolong it by the reminder of the research commitment. Some commentators have made the assertion that women may never (the less truthful say 'do never') get over rape, and information given by women about experiences years past in their lives can support this. All we know about, however, are the first few months – and *that* research has shown us that this can be plenty of time for women to feel they have got over the experience of rape.

DEVELOPING THE STUDY

When I first began to work on the issue of rape there seemed little of use around, except the discussion papers and ideas of some of the other women writers who had taken up the question of rape, the work on psychological profiles of rapists and other sex offenders, and Amir's Book *Patterns of Forcible Rape* (1971). A paper by Kurt Weis and Sandra Borges entitled 'Victimology and rape: The case of the legitimate victim' (1973), which looked at how rape comes into the dating relationship and discussed the control of situations and people's expectations, then led me to focus on the situation from which rape developed, at the types of situation women found themselves in and how they affected women's views of their own experiences.

As the research on rape expanded, especially work concerned with the effects of rape either on women as individuals or on a more political level, the details of what happened during the act itself became less important than how women received them. The combination of the focus on the 'pre-rape' situation and the attention shown to reactions and responses after rape put the act in its place in the overall process of victimisation. Moving on with that process, the idea of the patterns of response put forward by Sutherland and Scherl and Burgess and Holmstrom provided for me a structure within which to look at individual reactions to try to see what women were saying with them. Also, I too could see a clear difference between a 'crisis' period and the later period in victimisation where women are learning to cope with it. I saw the difference in part as a reactive/crisis time and an active/coping time.

The emphasis within the support services on giving women back the self-control they lost during the rape itself made control an important element to look at. This led into a focus on other people's reactions, because others could either support or take over in trying to help.

The psychological profiles of rapists, the categories of assault developed from rapists' accounts, police records and women's accounts, as a backdrop to the information I was gathering from the women I worked with, finally helped me to look at how important it was to see how women themselves define what has happened to them and how that influences their response to victimisation. I didn't see great relevance to raped women in defining rape by what type of assault takes place, or the actions and motives of the rapists. Types of assault may have legal and sociological interest, and it is vital for treatment and prevention programmes to understand men's actions, but my concern was to provide some insight into the effects of rape, and how women dealt with the whole process of victimisation.

The political writings of the early 1970s of Susan Brownmiller, Susan Griffin and Janice Reynolds were a big influence on me, as inspiration and as a source of ideas. Perhaps the biggest, though least definable, influence was the changing social consciousness about rape and the real experience of learning about all of this within the Anti-Rape Campaign itself. These combined over time with the academic theorising, the work of the support services, work in other (related) areas and the process of research itself, to structure my own work. Working within the Campaign meant learning about research in a specifically feminist atmosphere, and so the development of feminist research was another part of the background to this study.

WORKING AT FEMINIST RESEARCH

At the end of my MA year, a member of the department asked me how I could consider myself a sociologist when I had spent a whole year studying 'nothing but women'. He had walked away before I closed my mouth, registered the insult and thought of an answer. I thought that I had spent time looking at important social issues like rape and abortion, and believed that I had worked at developing an approach to the subject (and subjects) which was sensitive and valid for the chosen viewpoint – that of women. With his comment I had to confront head-on the fact that I was ignoring the views of half the population. That, in itself, was not the problem: he had presumably done the same thing in his work, but I had chosen the wrong half to ignore. This was my glaring example of the 'sexism in sociology' discussed by Ann Oakley (1985) in her book *The Sociology of Housework* and is shared here as a part of the ongoing debate about the need for a specific feminist approach to social research.

A second problem came up when I was actually preparing the study of women's responses to rape. It was suggested that, to ensure a balanced picture, I should look at rapists too. I couldn't, frankly, see the point. Even were I stupid enough to ask the women whom I had been working with for permission to seek out and find the men who had raped them, what those men could tell me about how women responded to rape seemed somewhat sparse. If I were not to interview the men who had attacked the women in the study, then finding any bunch of rapists seemed even less relevant. What was being applied was a blanket judgement on research methods and aims not connected with the actual subject matter or situation at all. Balance, just for a while, became a confused word for me.

Sociology has existed for too long with the idea that the study of men and male behaviour is really the study of society, and that women come up in the relevant places such as the study of the family. The increased interest born of the Women's Liberation Movement in the study of women in their own right was seen as highly specialised, highly partial, unbalanced and biased. Finding myself in such an interesting side-shoot of sociology, I turned to the work of other feminist writers to see how they defined the words, and so my work.

The complaints that feminist researchers had against social studies as a whole were focused on several levels of work. On the wider theoretical level, social science, which claimed to be starting from a completely objective standpoint, was in fact just taking the status quo as base and so was taking on board all the myths, assumptions and prejudices that society holds. Along with others working in such areas as race and class, or looking at the sociology of 'development', feminists said that social studies took a 'Western, christian, white, professional, class-biased standpoint, saying 'this is normal, this is interesting, we will measure everything else against it'. This, argued the 'everything else', was not being objective but taking a conservative political stand. In part, the problem was seen as what was not said as much as what was.

As always, language became crucial (Spender, 1977). If 'man' is assumed to mean 'people', then the fact that there is a distinct difference in the way that male and female are created by society is ignored. It also means that 'woman' becomes something other than 'people'; non-existent in fact. So, one of the first tasks for feminists within social sciences was to make women more visible, but not just to say 'women do this too'. The point needed to be made that the study of women would shed new light, provide new information, on society as a whole. For example, in *Women, Crime and Society*, Eileen B. Leonard comments:

> Women are typically noncriminal: they have lower rates of crime in all nations, all communities within nations, for all age groups, for all periods of recorded history, and for practically all crimes. Still, this intriguing and significant information has been left un-examined.

> (Leonard, 1982, Preface)

For a first step, then, a sociology of women. However, there were already signs of what could happen to such a sociology. Where women had been studied, albeit as social roles such as 'mothers' or 'wives', women's actions could be separated out and marginalised. Although welcomed as a start and an opening up of vast areas of interesting work, Women's Studies could, it was feared, end up the poor relation of social science. As long as the sociology of men is called simply 'sociology', the sociology of women is reduced and marginalised, for stating clearly what it is.

What was needed, feminists argued, was in fact a sociology for women – not just a first step, but a new focus on women's experiences and situation which would develop fresh approaches, attitudes and methods for social research, where the particulars of women's existence would be understood and catered for. Brought out from under the wing of a sociology of men and given an existence of its own, it was possible then to see a feedback into the system, a removal of masculine bias, and a development of a sociology which is human in perspective. At the moment, we are nowhere near completing the first step, if women's studies is that, and so cannot say whether sociologies based on gender differences which our society finds so important to maintain, recognise the knowledge which can be gained from studying the ignored half of the population, and also recognise that, in challenging the subject and subjects of research, methods and analysis may also change.

In developing a women-centred social studies, feminists, from the start, had to defend their own existence, with the conservative thinkers accusing them of a lack of objectivity and impartiality. As the offered wisdom of the critics such concepts needed careful handling. The idea of *objectivity*, for example, has divided social scientists from the early classic theorists onwards. To be 'objective' has been assumed to mean non-political, but this seems now to have been discarded as it becomes more and more obvious that 'non-political', especially when applied to studying society, is a meaningless term. It has often come up in the past as meaning conservative (i.e. that everything not conservative is 'political'), so 'objective' can be used to describe work that has no stated political perspective and no explanation of the position of the researcher. This, therefore, does not apply to feminist research, which acknowledges the politics in any understanding of the situation of women and, in claiming the title feminist, states also the basic position of the research.

A more valuable use of the idea of objectivity is that it can be taken to mean standing outside or aloof from the subject, assuming that all aspects of the action observed can be seen equally and studied dispassionately. That *a* valuable viewpoint is that of the observer is not in doubt, nor the fact that an outsider to a situation can provide new insight or can describe or analyse the action in a way that no-one involved can. The problem, for some research, is the assumption that the observer's view is the truth. This can then be imposed on the activity as its meaning, regardless of what the participants think or feel. In this way is the Expert created and the subjects become data sources. For the subjects, there is only received wisdom about their own experiences. For feminists, this approach mirrors the treatment of women by society. In creating a hierarchy within research which so closely resembles the hierarchy of society, feminists had to question where this approach had come from and why. While recognising the value of looking at a situation from outside it, focusing not on what it means to those involved but on the wider picture created, feminism also sees the necessity of adding personal experience and understanding to provide a full picture. If the view of the outsider is objective, then feminists argue that, for true balance, the objective viewpoint needs a touch of subjectivity.

Paul Rock (1973), in *Deviant Behavior*, makes a distinction between 'knowing about' and 'knowing', concepts which seem appropriate here. The 'stand aloof and uninvolved' approach to social studies may give us the information to 'know about' a subject, but from Howard Becker's question 'Whose side are we on?', asked in 1967 to the radical approaches to social studies which answer it clearly, the argument for involvement, of taking sides if necessary, and declaring an interest in the subject, has been that it is the only way of 'knowing' a subject well.

Again, with *impartiality* as with objectivity, we run into the difficulties with social studies which are ambiguous. While some research is falsely assumed to be impartial, because the particular biases of the method, aim and personnel have not been stated, the work which is honest in its approach appears less generalised and so reflectively more biased. Standing as an objective observer, and commenting on what I found as an impartial reviewer of social science methods, I would rather spend my time looking at results which are clearly defined than have to work out the bias of an unstated interest.

Objectivity and impartiality had to be confronted in my own work from theory right through to what questions to ask, and when and how to ask them.

To begin with, in looking at rape, it seemed most sensible to recognise that the same act is experienced differently, depending on the roles of those involved. The rapist may experience it as sex, the raped woman as violence, and the observer or recorder experiences nothing of the act except the reflected accounts of those involved. There is nothing which can make an understanding of rape less subjective or partial. It is an experience, experiences are essentially subjective, and each person involved can only describe it partially. So, feminist research provided a structure within which to explore the subjectivity and so understand the subject better. It was also clear that just as 'men' meant 'people' within sociology as a whole so the male understanding of rape was being taken as the 'reality'. Women's experiences had to be taken from the sidelines and made a central concern.

I understood these issues through my work in general. As a counsellor, the ability to listen and respond to a woman's experience without becoming overwhelmed by it was an essential part of my work and training, but I could never see this as being objective. I am not outside or aloof from the subject, because I am involved in a relationship with the woman who is sharing her account, and do not remain unaffected by it. Further, as a feminist counsellor, an essential part of my understanding of the relationship was that, although more powerful because I can control the interaction and have knowledge the other woman may not have, it is essential that I can understand her situation and, to some extent, see myself in it. For this study, although a broader viewpoint may have been lost, it seemed more valuable to base research on the relationship which allowed a woman safely to relate her experiences, which shared to some extent the process of change which she was going through and which already was meant to analyse and understand her situation. Instead of fighting with a methodology which denied the value of the counselling relationship, and which would have meant filtering out information and insights rather than use them, I found comfort in the work of women like Liz Stanley and Sue Wise who could write:

> Because the basis of all research is a relationship, this necessarily involves the presence of the researcher *as a person*. Personhood cannot be left out of the research process. And so we insist that it must be capitalised upon, it must be made full use of.
> (Stanley and Wise, 1983, p. 162)

Again, as a feminist counsellor involved in the Anti-Rape Campaign, the issue of control meant that I took the issue of personal involvement further than my own role. I saw my work as a backdrop or guidance for women who needed, temporarily, some extra support in dealing with their immediate situation and past experience. In some ways, the support was passive – a handrail not needed for most of the steps taken. Another function was more active, and that was to reflect a woman's situation back to her, in a form she could use constructively to create change or comfort for herself. I saw the research process in a similar way – in part, a passive absorption of information, a working with the subjects to create and interpret the knowledge gained, and also a reflection of what was learned. What was rejected in counselling, as in research, was the supremacy of the expert outsider who alone could interpret the subject and provide a solution.

There was one final connection to be made between the general issues raised by feminist research and the specific study of rape. One problem with social research methods is that they could deny subjectivity and so reduce the analysis of human relations to measured functions, and reduce those studied to objects. As feminism saw this as only a reflection of social attitudes to women generally, so I could see parallels with rape itself. Rape is the turning of a woman into an object for the rapist's use only. There is no relationship, but an empty function between the rapist and the raped. It seemed untenable then to take on research methods which reflected such a process, for the process of objectification itself seemed as objectionable as victimisation. Feminist research allowed an exploration of women's experiences, allowed their subjectivity – and allowed the research process to challenge and transcend the oppression it was in some ways studying. It was a positive background to my own work.

IN THE BEGINNING . . .

My involvement with the Anti-Rape Campaign started in 1974 and came about through my work as a pregnancy counsellor. I knew through talking to women about their decisions to seek abortions that their feelings about the sexual relationship which had resulted in pregnancy affected their response to the experience of abortion. Two women I saw for counselling for abortion worried me in particular. Both had been raped, one by a stranger, the other by a close friend. For both, the abortion was far less of a problem to them than their feelings about themselves and the rape. I felt useless to them, unable to offer any real support or constructive advice because I knew nothing about rape – other than the fact that it was an issue which concerned American feminists.

Talking to another counsellor about how I felt, she gave me details of a meeting called by an English doctor, Judy Gilley, who had worked with a Rape Crisis Centre in the US. I went to that meeting hoping for some information which would help me in my own counselling – expecting, I suppose, the transferred wisdom of the experts to be passed down the chain as I was used to. Instead, what was understood was that there were no experts on rape, only women who needed support and those of us who could pool our skills in giving it – recognising always that we could be both. So, I became part of the group who set up the London Rape Crisis Centre.

The first year of the group was spent in setting up – finding premises, funding, and using whatever resources we could think of (and who would work with us) as training aids for developing counselling skills and a support service. Research into women's reactions to rape, of which there was little at the time, was seen as a development of self-training. We went through other people's work, used our own experiences, and developed ways of monitoring our own work – always to feed the gathered information and insight back into the support networks themselves.

The RCC in London opened in March 1976, uncomfortably housed, with shaky finances and a small number of committed workers and volunteers. There were also a small number of women who had made contact and asked for support, despite no publicity and the great suspicion surrounding this odd little group. We were told time and time again that rape wasn't a problem in England; we weren't needed. We didn't believe it then, and women now working in support services around the country know from their own experiences that it is not true. It was within this context of scepticism from 'out there', and an intense need to know, that I registered for a PhD, entitled, 'Victimisation through rape'.

Between 1976 and 1978 was a period of intense activity for the study as well as the Centre itself. Those of us involved with the Centre were running the twenty-four-hour phone line, training new volunteers, providing legal, medical and emotional support, publicising the Centre and the needs of raped women, fund-raising and, wherever possible, trying to be helpful to new groups starting up. To some extent, the needs of the Centre out-weighed the needs of the research, except that the two were closely linked – if the Centre collapsed, so did the research. The research could have disappeared, but was useful in providing space to look at what we were doing, and in gathering the grow-ing number of information sources.

In the first two and a half years, somewhere between 200 and 250 women contacted the Centre. Because of the smallness of the collective (between six and ten women), it was possible – in fact, necessary – for me as a counsellor to have some information about all calls and contacts, from which the final illustrative sample gradually evolved. This wider scope of information was vital, because it allowed the study to progress within a frame-work of broader experience, so that information gained could continually be measured against other information; patterns looked for and checked; ideas tested out to see if they really did mean anything at all. As work progressed in the US too, it was possible to get a view of the research as an overall exploration into the responses and needs of raped women. Some patterns of response were beginning to emerge, as well as common factors identified, which helped to understand the experience of victim-isation – for example, the issue of control was clearly important whether in looking at rape experience itself (and the effect of having control taken away from you), or at responses and who controlled how women responded to victimisation through rape.

By the middle of 1978, I began to feel a limitation in looking at personal responses in isolation from the support which was allowing women to talk about their experiences. Women con-tacting the RCC were not just repeating their accounts for the benefit of research, but were going through a process of change and were actively supported when doing so. The women's experiences, therefore, had to be understood in the context of that process and the role the RCC played in it. One interesting observation was how control once again loomed large in under-standing, because it was apparent that who controlled the public responses to rape, i.e. whether feminist or not, made a big difference to what those responses were, and what attitudes were directing support to raped women.

My attention shifted then towards the Anti-Rape Campaign itself and eventually towards a study of women's *political* responses to victimisation through rape. 'The personal is political' took on a new meaning for me, as the interaction of women's personal responses, and the public or political responses, became interwoven. Although the political responses eventually became a separate study, the connections between the two remain always, particularly in the counselling and support services at the heart of the political campaign. The counselling relationship itself is structured and informed by the political campaign, but is a personal response to individual victimisation. In another way, support services are also the point at which personal distress is brought into the public sphere, and becomes a political issue.

Between 1978 and 1980, I stopped counselling within the RCC, and by 1980 had stopped being a member of the collective, confronting for myself the issue of 'burn out', where commitment to work or action may not diminish, but the ability to be effective does. I needed, along with some of the other women who had been involved, to stand back from rape and become involved in other issues. I continued, on and off, as a counsellor in other work, still seeing women who had been raped and thus adding to the wealth of experience, still continually analysing responses. Instead of an active participant in the Anti-Rape Campaign, I became an observer, closer to the 'passive action' usually associated with research, but still in many ways involved.

THINKING AND DOING – THE RESEARCH ITSELF

The theory behind the research

When looking at women's personal responses to rape, the basic belief behind the study was that the act of rape is only a part of a process of victimisation which begins prior to the act that we know of as rape, and continues with the situation and experiences a woman goes through in responding to the act.

This process of victimisation is directly related to the feminist analysis of rape, which is that it is not necessarily the result of individual pathology, but that the roots lie in 'normal' male–female relations where women as a social group are objectified.

In particular, the polarisation of the genders into separate and opposing feminine and masculine ideals provides a role model for women which contains the potential for victimisation and, for men, one which contains the potential for victimising. It was too much for this one study to try to prove the relationship between the gender role models and individual acts of rape, but the assumption that human activity is influenced by gender role models was used to analyse the 'normal' situations women and men found themselves in and from which the act of rape developed. In the study, these are called the 'pre-rape' situations.

When the process of victimisation was under study, it became clear that it was important to recognise and understand women's actions. The term and idea of 'victim precipitation' was rejected as an after-the-event justification and a rapist's understanding, but it was always possible to go to the other extreme and assume a woman's total passivity and so ignore the real decisions and action with which she was involved. Only in recognising the women's activity in responding to rape was it possible to get any idea of what is meant to them.

One term which has to be defined for this research is 'victim'. The theoretical base of the study saw 'being a victim' as a socially defined role or status, attained by (or forced on) an individual or group through specific acts or beliefs of others – the victimisers. For understanding women's responses to rape I felt that it was vital to keep to the fore the maxim that being a victim is only a part of being a person. At the start of the research, I saw 'being a victim' as one type of social role, with fairly commonly understood indicators of what the role was. By the end, my view was that 'being a victim' is not one role, but one of many possible types of role, i.e. that there is more than one type of victim. Because of this development, the study was specifically concerned with the extent to which women accepted victim status, what types of victimisation they saw themselves as suffering, and how this influenced their responses.

Leading on from this, there was the question of other people's view of victimisation, and how this influenced women's responses and the choices open to them. It was another theoretical assumption that, if women through socialisation tend to see themselves reflectively, through others' eyes, the attitude and reaction of others would be important in the process of victimisation. So, other people's expectations of a 'victim's' behaviour

was looked at alongside women's feelings about others' responses, and also in terms of who controlled the situations the
women were in before, during and after the rape. Included as
'relevant others' are the RCC personnel the woman came into
contact with. By doing this, the effect of support could be
monitored as well as an awareness of the wider, public, response
to rape which also had its own influence on how women felt
about their own experiences.

Information gathering

When starting this study, I was faced with collecting information about something which there was patchy knowledge of –
women's responses to rape. I was also treating the information I
was given in two ways. As a researcher, my need was to have
clear information relevant to the study: as a counsellor, I was
also looking at that information in terms of the woman's own
needs, including the need to give information only as it suited
her. The intention at first had been to conduct 'interviews',
using a format to collect information in a set sequence, asking
the same questions of each woman. This proved both impossible
and, in the long run, wasteful. When the interviews were tried,
the women, although they said it had been useful, were distressed and needed extra support and counselling – not an experience to be repeated more than the twice it occurred. Part of the
problem was the time, but mainly it was the cold recollection, in
an imposed order, of painful experiences and feelings. The interview also seemed to me to belong to research into something in
the past or something static, or where the need is to catch one
moment of time. Women's responses were part of a process, and
one interview, even coupled with notes taken over a period of
time, could only address the issues relevant to the woman at
that time. As the results of the study will show, even the way
women described their experience of rape could change over
time, depending on what aspect concerned them most at a
particular time. With all these considerations, I looked around
for a more flexible, but structured approach.

   Two books, describing the same method, finally gave me a
way forward. *The Discovery of Grounded Theory* by Barney
Glaser and Anselm Strauss (1975) suggested in grounded
theory an approach which would give a structure to deal with a

process rather than an act. With grounded theory, the data is assembled through a combination of formal methods of collection, random choices of direction and 'insight' or 'inspiration' – which is normally unacknowledged but is a part of most research which is innovative.

Kristin Luker (1975), in *Taking Chances: Abortion and the Decision not to Contracept* (1975) had also used grounded theory because she wanted the space to develop ideas with the structure to guide her work. The other part of her work I was interested in was her use of the idea of 'rational decision-making' within what most professionals would have termed risk-taking, i.e. having unprotected intercourse without wanting conception. She used a type of 'cost–benefit' analysis to look at the accounts of the women she interviewed. I found the idea (suitably adapted) appealing for my own work, because rational decision-making steered clear of the assumption that women were totally passive, and the 'cost–benefit' idea gave some substance to the reasoning women would employ in deciding how to act and how to respond. These approaches and constructs became for me the guidelines for my work.

Instead of an interview where both the woman and myself would have to cope with the research demands, the ordering of information was done purely in the notes. At the heart of the order were checklists for each of the women who agreed that her information could be used for research. Broadly, the information kept was: personal details, the pre-rape situation, the rape itself, immediate post-rape situation, physical effects, feelings/experiences over time, and details of all contacts. Apart from these checklists, journals were kept. One was a basic diary of events, including the progress of the research, when women were contacted, and public or political events. Other journals followed up issues brought up by the women, or drawn from the literature. Overall, information was gathered from counselling sessions, counsellors' notes, meetings, discussions, letters, interviews, literature and observation. There was always the possibility of contacting individual women to clarify or add to information, and this was done occasionally, when the information was easy or it clearly would not cause distress to make contact. It was important for this study that the work was done alongside, and as part of, research on public responses to rape, because it kept the world outside, ever one of the influences on

the women, always in mind. What came out of the whole
research process was an insight into how women understood
their own victimisation through rape, and who or what they
used to help them cope.

3 THE PROCESS OF RAPE

It's not the strangeness which is most frightening about being raped, it's how horribly normal it is.

(Anon)

We usually think of rape as a single act, sudden and contained. The accounts of women who have been raped show us that rape goes on well after that one act, as they try to cope with the experience. When discussing the attitude of the police and courts, the early criticism of the criminal justice system was that it put women through a 'second rape', with the hostile questioning and reduction of women to victim-witnesses. This was a clear example of the factors after the fact which can make a difference to the overall experience.

In talking to women about what happened to them, and in looking at the roots of rape, it was soon made clear that the process of victimisation through rape can, in practice and in theory, begin before the act of rape itself. To understand the personal experience of rape, it was necessary to look at how it had come about.

The *pre-rape* situation acts as a starting point, or the cross-over between before and after victimisation. Such situations are only marked as different because of what followed from them, not because any aspect could be isolated at the time they were happening. It is the situation which the rapist uses to isolate or gain access to the woman he intends to rape. That intention may develop during the pre-rape situation (i.e. it is opportunistic) or be apparent well before.

The *assault* initiates victimisation and starts really at the point where the woman realises the true meaning of the situation and acknowledges to herself that the rapist intends to rape her. The end of the situation is marked by the separation of the woman from her assailant(s). The ending alone can greatly influence a woman's reactions and choices later.

The *post-rape* situation is the critical decision-making time. Initially this was judged as the time until the woman slept, but this was not always relevant as women could extend the time they needed to sort out, literally, what to do next. It is the true crisis period.

Coping, or more than coping, was what followed – the longer-term response where the experience of rape is taken into life, where victimisation is dealt with, where women decide what has happened to them and where, eventually, rape becomes history. There can be elements of crisis for the woman in this stage too. Injuries or continued vulnerability can leave the woman feeling the assault itself is not over. Repeated assaults can re-create the crisis period time and time again. Other factors, such as a court case, or discovery of pregnancy, or first experience of sexual activity after the rape, can at times 'throw' the woman's attempts at coping and dealing with the rape in her life.

As well as the passage of time through the process, there are different levels on which victimisation works. At the most *public* level there is the definition of 'victim' laid on by others and taken on by the woman as a kind of 'social identity'. The social identity consists of common understandings of rape and 'being a victim', the ideas carried around by friends, relatives and processed through the media and myths. The social identity of 'victim' exists for the woman, whether anyone is really told about the experience or not. In a sense, it is what will be expected of her by herself and others. Erving Goffman (1963), writing about 'stigma' or dealing with factors which set some apart from others as 'different', talks about the 'management of a spoilt identity'. The low opinion society has of victims ensures that a 'spoilt identity' is exactly what 'being a victim' is.

Bringing the level a step closer, a woman has to make decisions about how public she will make her own experience. Dealing on an *inter-personal* level, the actions and reactions of those around her become part of the whole process and something the woman has to deal with, even if she deals with it without actually involving anyone. For example, a woman may decide not to tell her mother because she believes her mother will be upset and only make matters worse. In taking that decision, she is looking at the inter-personal level of the process and making choices about how to handle it. Equally, the public level can be brought in here, if decisions about who to involve and why hinge on what the others may think about rape or victimisation. The decision whether or not to involve the police may well carry considerations about the police attitude to rape and women who report it. The counselling relationship also works on this inter-personal level, and is one example of an involvement of another which has specific influences on how the woman responds to her experience and how she can use the support of others. Because counselling was developed on the public level, as part of the feminist anti-rape movement, it is another way that the public level is brought in.

Counselling also involves the *personal* level, where the woman sorts the various experiences, feelings, situations and reactions into her own response. Kristin Luker (1975), in work on women making choices about contraception and abortion, used the idea of 'rational decision-making' which applies a cost–benefit analysis to choices and actions which are very often thought of as unthinking or irrational – like taking chances with contraception. The idea was that women weigh up the pros and cons of actions but use their own view of their situation rather than the view of others around. Just as this gave a clearer understanding of women's understanding of their own contraception and fertility control, so such an approach allows a different aspect of responding to victimisation to come through. The personal level of response is not a passive acceptance of the act or uncontrolled reactions to it, but an active assessment and decision-making process. In this way, seemingly irrational or counter-productive actions can be seen from the point of view of the woman herself, and understanding her reasoning. The oft-quoted complaint from the police about women reporting rape concerns the ones who have a bath or shower before reporting, thereby losing valuable evidence. To follow the logic of criminal justice, the woman must see herself first and foremost as a prosecution witness or piece of evidence, and react accordingly. What she may actually see herself as is someone who has been dirtied by the rape and the first priority, for her peace of mind, may well be to be cleansed. It is the woman who feels and not the police witness who is responding at this point, and for her the response is rational.

Before the process of victimisation is looked at by going through the situations in time, it is useful to begin by looking at the women themselves, or at least at information about their lives which they used, on the personal level of response, to help themselves. Factors such as age, background, lifestyle, situation and personality added up or combined into points they could draw on when deciding appropriate responses. Such factors were not necessarily useful in determining whether or not they were raped, though some could be used by the rapists to increase vulnerability, but their importance was in how the women themselves saw the factors and how they related them to victimisation.

THE WOMEN THEMSELVES

Information about the women themselves has been used in past studies to indicate what can increase women's vulnerability to rape or to refute common sense notions about who gets raped. However useful such information is, in giving support to women who have been raped, it is no comfort to say they are (or are not) typical 'victims'. The concern here is to look at factors which may influence how a woman deals with the rape experience.

Although the usual information such as age, occupation, civil status, etc., was collected, it was soon clear, from this and other work, that such information alone would not be of much help. The standard socio-economic indicators hardly work for women, and were not designed for us. Employment is no indicator of a woman's class background, and class itself has different connotations both between the sexes and between different areas or countries. It was apparent, however, that background or lifestyle did influence how a woman understood her experience, as different backgrounds provided different supports or problems. Talking to women about their lives indicated some aspects which had been used by them in coping with the assault and response, and also indicated others which were clearly used by the rapist to manipulate the situation. These are looked at later. To get an idea of background and lifestyle, various factors were combined to give a picture of women's lives and their situation at the time of the rape. The women themselves saw their age, occupation, housing and area of residence as having a bearing

on their responses to the experience of rape and how they dealt
with it (Table 3.1).

Table 3.1 The parameters of background (at time of assault)

Age	No.	Occupation	No.	Housing	No.	Area of residence	No.
10–19	9	Unemployed	6	With family	16	London	18
20–29	16	Student	10	Flat share	4	Home Counties	7
30–39	2	Secretarial	4	Flat alone	5	Other	5
40–49	3	Mother	4	Squat	3		
Other	6			Other	2		

Age – by excluding experiences of rape in childhood (under
ten years), the emphasis here is on teenage and young adult
women, whom several studies have indicated are the ones most
vulnerable, not only to rape, but to all serious victimisation.
Age alone was of little importance to the women, except that it
gave a lead into such factors as the type of social situations
which women would have been expected to be in, or dependency
on others or possible support networks which could be used.

Occupation was a measure which on the surface had little
value but affected other issues. For example, lack of paid work
could indicate dependency on others, which influenced who had
to be told. Having a job could mean that women had a routine
they had to keep to, introducing normality and giving a place
they had to cope in. Work places could also represent friends and
possible supporters. Only ten of the thirty women had jobs
which gave them an independent income, which meant that
possible responses which entailed spending money were limited
for the other twenty. For example, in the US studies, women
after a rape experience were shown to move house at a higher
rate than average. Lack of a job or a job which was tied to a
particular area, or a move dependent on another financing it,
certainly meant for this group of women that moving home,
even if they had wanted to, was often out of the question, except
for those who were planning to move, or those in insecure
housing such as squats.

Housing was a way of finding out who the women lived with
and who, therefore, might be close at hand to be involved. Half
the women were living with families, either as a dependent
child or as a mother. These therefore had relations immediately

at hand to turn to, and the other half of the women had friends. This did not show the type of relationship, or the likelihood of a woman getting valuable support, but pointed the way and gave a structure to the step of looking at who else was involved and why.

How women felt about their *area of residence* had a considerable influence on their feelings of security and how they responded to having their security shaken by the rape. Twelve of the women living in London came from areas that were considered 'run down' but only three of them said that they were worried about the neighbourhood. For the others, it was clear that they were aware of potential hassles but not unduly concerned. Those in the suburbs felt that they had no need to worry. Those travelling felt they were taking reasonable precautions: one who was travelling had been very careful when out on her own and was raped in hospital. For most of the women, then, the rapes came as a considerable blow to their feelings of security and peace of mind in everyday matters. Four women were raped in areas away from their homes – two of them abroad and two in the UK. Tied in with other factors, this shaking of confidence in the normal pattern of life was a major issue concerned with the victimisation which the women had to deal with.

This idea of background gives some indication of where the women were in their lives at the time of the rape and hints at issues which would come up later in the process. More than these factors though, were experiences of life which women saw as being relevant to their experience of rape, and what their lives felt like at the time the rape occurred.

Table 3.2 Specific problems mentioned

Problem/experience stated	No.
Emotional/psychological (treatment given)	6
Family conflicts	6
Marriage/relationship	
ended	4
under strain	2
Loneliness	2
Drug abuse (hard drugs)	2
Physical disability	2
Trouble with police	2

When specific incidents in the past were mentioned, it was often in connection with something which happened in the rape or how they felt. Comments would start with 'It's like what happened when . . .'. Sixteen of the women mentioned a variety of issues from their past which they saw as important (Table 3.2).

Obviously, the problems or incidents were clustered differently for each woman and were used in different ways. In talking about things from the past, and what was happening around the time of the rape, an idea of lifestyle emerged, based on how the women saw the paths of their lives developing. As rough labels, three descriptions were used (Table 3.3).

Table 3.3 Lifestyle and specific problems mentioned

Lifestyle	No.	Problems
Secure	18	3
Stable now	7	8
Unstable	5	5

A *secure* lifestyle was outlined by those women who felt comfortable with their lives and suggested an acceptable pattern or model until the rape – 'as it should be' was how one woman explained it. There had been few problems or crises to deal with, and any that had come up had been smoothly sorted out. Two issues were important here. The first was that some women found that their lives held nothing to prepare them for the violence, the lack of control and the abuse they then experienced and the rape then hit hard at that security and the trust they had in themselves and their lives. The second point which came out was that, conversely, women could draw on the confidence that such security gave them, and use their lives and those around them for support:

Enid was working abroad, her 'adventure' before settling down to a suitable career and suitable marriage. Her family were well off, an ideal image of the middle class, and very supportive of each other. When she was raped, **Enid** immediately felt that she had been so utterly debased that she couldn't fit into her nice, clean family any more. At first she refused to return home, then when she did she withdrew into herself and refused to let her family in on her experience or pain in any way.

Sara was a teenager from a happy, comfortably-off family, with a steady job, steady boyfriend and plenty of friends. When she was raped, her reaction was confusion – 'why me? I've never hurt anyone, never mixed with rough people, never been in trouble. Why couldn't they leave me alone?' Her mother was ill at the time she was raped, so she didn't tell her family immediately what had happened. She did tell friends and from them and the unknowing family too, she drew strength and never felt that the rape had changed her or showed her to be wrong or bad in any way. Her life helped her to focus the blame on the rapists.

The women who described their lives as *stable now* felt that after a period of upset or disturbance they had finally achieved some kind of order and stability – things were finally working out for them. Their security, therefore, was fragile and the rape experience brought fears that they would be thrown back into less happy times. Although they had experience of problems, they were in one sense as unprepared for victimisation as those women who had not. They saw themselves and their lives as changed and the rape belonged to the bad old days, not the new:

Terri was settling into a new life alone with a small baby after getting away from a violent husband. She lived in what was recognised as a rough estate, but had her family around her and was managing. The rape experience challenged her confidence in living alone and managing her life for herself.

Anni had also once been married to a violent man, and had struggled to regain her confidence and security away from him. She had married again, this time a very gentle man whose support was vital to her. The past violence made her want to avoid any kind of conflict, but when it came she was able to use her new security as well as an old anger to help her get through.

Where *unstable* was the most apt description for a woman's lifestyle, there was conversely a kind of security in evidence. In an insecure existence, women expected nothing to go right and were almost resigned to conflicts and problems. Often the response to the rape was eventually to take it on board as one more hassle in their lives. This is not to say, however, that the experience hurt them any less than other women; for the women who saw themselves in an unstable situation, the rape at first seemed the last straw:

Olivia was living in a squat, a heroin addict who had been in and out of children's homes most of her life. She had survived by using the welfare and social service agencies, but never let anyone get close enough to make an impression on her. The one security she had was a trust in the others in her situation and circle, based on a belief that the ones to be wary of were the rest of a society which she didn't really belong to. She was raped by a man she knew and was thrown into a period of total disruption but eventually she just dropped out of sight and reappeared in another squat, with new people around – she had put the rape in the past and started again.

Jo, on the surface, seemed to be in a perfectly stable situation, but such is the strength of the myth of the English middle classes. She had rebelled as a teenager and married young to a man her family didn't like. The marriage had been stormy and was in the final stages of ending when she was raped. She had put up with a lifestyle and living standards she couldn't have imagined in her childhood and which she realised she actually hated. The rape experience came at a time when she was questioning everything she had done in the past, and what she would do in the future. Her comment was 'I don't want to live in a world that's painful, loud and violent, but I am'.

In connecting background, lifestyle and the experience of rape, previous experiences of many types showed themselves to be relevant. The idea of background and lifestyle provide the backdrop against which women understood their lives, while particular experiences in the past helped to define just what the rape meant. An immediate and obvious connection could be made with previous experiences of sex, or violence, or both.

Sex wasn't asked about as a problem in the past, though it was sometimes mentioned in that context. Although the experience of rape is violent, it can also be felt as an attack on sexuality, and it certainly uses sex as a weapon. Previous sexual experience has sometimes been used to distinguish the 'innocent' from the woman who cannot really be raped – because researchers, as much as others, can fall into the trap of implying that women who have an active sex life give up the right ever to refuse. When looking at response, the assumption has also been made that rape is 'worse' for a woman who has had no sexual experience. Neither removing responsibility for the attack from the rapist nor giving measures of severity to the experience throw any light on what difference previous sexual experience makes to how a woman deals with rape in her own life. There were two questions asked by the women themselves. The first was how their own experiences would influence how they dealt with the rape, and the second was how the rape would leave them feeling about sex. What sex meant to them, what they got from it, and what associations other than sexual pleasure it had for them were, in the light of their own understanding, relevant issues (Table 3.4).

Table 3.4 Previous sexual experience

Experience	No.
Unsatisfactory	
within relationship	5
casual	5
Good experience overall	14
None	6

Iris had had no sexual experience when she was raped. She had been brought up to believe that sex was a gift and only good and right within a marriage. Her mother had given a clear impression that sex was, in fact, a duty. The rape was brutal, humiliating and left Iris with a feeling that she had been spoilt and would never know sex unsullied by rape again.

Sara also had had no sexual experience, but had talked about it with her boyfriend and both had decided to wait until they really felt it was right for them. She never connected the rape with her feelings with her boyfriend and was only concerned that, when they did finally make love, it would hurt her as the rape had.

Alice had been married and found sex unsatisfactory with her husband. She didn't like penetration at all and only began to enjoy sex when she began a lesbian relationship. She felt that her dislike of penetration made the rape worse and also found that the violence of the rape affected her feelings about her lover, which upset both of them.

Hilda had an easy and open attitude towards sex and didn't initially connect her rape experience and sex at all. After some months, she said that she had started to rethink some of her attitudes towards sex and felt that sometimes her previous relationships had contained elements of rape in them. This made her more wary of relationships she felt were oppressive or uncomfortable, but not wary of sex in itself.

Patience was raped in her early teens and connected her later problems with sex back to the experience and her parents' attitude. In her childhood home, sex had been a battleground and her parents, when told about the rape, had effectively ignored it. She felt sex as a looming and threatening presence in her life, and couldn't relate to her husband's attitude which she saw as insensitive – sex was important to him and he couldn't connect his sexuality with her experience of rape at all.

Norma had come through a broken marriage and was very lonely. She relied on male company a great deal and sex was to her a reward to them for their attention to her. The rape cut her off from male company because she didn't trust them, and men had been her social lifeline. Her sexual experience was less important to her than the social and emotional comfort she had been getting and was no longer able to get, after the rape.

Bea saw no problems in the sexual relationship she had enjoyed for years with her husband and was determined that the rape would not spoil it. She was prepared to wait a while after the rape before she resumed her sexual life, because she wanted to maintain a distance from the rape. In a way, she saw the need for a recovery period, but no more.

In looking at the sexual experiences of women, an important part of how sex was affected by the rape was how others responded to the woman's needs, and thus was connected clearly with the support possible from others. How women related the rape to their sexual lives depended a great deal on what sex had meant to them anyway, either as a reality or as an idea.

Violence in a woman's past was an even clearer connection with rape. For eight out of the thirteen women who described their lives as either 'unstable' or 'stable now', getting away from violence had either caused disruption or played a major part in it. For them, the violence of the rape was both a reminder and a threat – that one act could cause another painful period of their lives. Violence in the past came mainly within the home environment (Table 3.5):

Table 3.5 Incidents of violence

Violence	No.	Sexual assault	No.
From male partner	5		
Within family	2	= Father	2
Other	3	= Other	3
Self inflicted	1		

Clearly, for five of the women, violence from their own previous experience was connected with sexual assault. How the previous experience had been handled made a difference to how the women related it to rape:

Lianne was in a children's home as a result of her father raping her. The case had gone to court and she hated the police, officials and her father for putting her through such an experience. The overwhelming feeling she had was anger, a determination not to be used again.
Yvonne had also ended up in a children's home because of assaults from her father and brother. She felt she had been blamed for breaking up the family home when her father went to prison and was easily made to feel guilty about prosecuting the rapist. She expressed a fear which came up with other women who had been taken out of the family home for their own safety – that the result of them making their rape public would be that, once again, they would be 'put away'.

The fact that violence was associated with the home for those women who had experienced it influenced what potential support they felt they could call on – they couldn't turn for help to those who had already victimised them.

Sexual or other physical violence was only one area where previous experiences of violence of a sort were related to the rape. Along with child sexual abuse there was also an emotional violence where the young women would be made to feel that they were at fault, either guilty of causing their own pain or disrupting the lives of others. One young woman (not in this study) whose mother had suffered from depression for years, was made to feel she had caused her own father's death because she had not been capable of giving her mother the support she felt she needed and deserved. The father had died of cancer, but the overall effect was to make her feel that she was capable, without doing anything, of causing harm to others or, as in the rape, making people harm her. She couldn't turn to her family when she needed them, because she expected them to say it was all her fault.

Una, in complete contrast, had a family which was close and loving, even in the face of adversity. She had been directly involved in her father's death. As a small child, she had been trapped for hours in a crashed car with a father she knew was dead. She talked about feeling totally out of control, and facing her own death, and related that to her feelings during the rape. After the accident, she had gone to pieces, and her family had allowed her to 'let go and work it out', but always assuring her that she was not to blame for the accident. She had got close to breaking point after the rape, and said she would give in when she got home and ask her family to allow her to go through the same process again – but this time knowing that she was doing it to gain strength.

These thirty women range from those whose lives were almost a stereotype of 'normal' family life, to those whose idea of security was a temporary roof over their heads and no immediate trouble with the 'authorities'. Of the younger ones, some were just emerging from childhood while others had already experienced lives that forty-year-olds would have difficulty coping with. In coping with rape, some had to hold down jobs or studies, had families to support or get support from, while others faced unemployment, bad housing or bad relationships. While some had no experience at all of sex, others saw in sex emotional reassurance, trouble, or pleasure.

The various factors which are involved in building a picture of background or lifestyle also influence the first step in the time progress of rape. A woman's situation within her lifestyle and background will influence who she is routinely surrounded by and the kinds of social situations she would be used to being involved in. Where the myth of rape places it outside our normal lives, the reality is that it develops from the kinds of situation all of us could find ourselves in.

THE PRE-RAPE SITUATION

There were four broad types of situation which the thirty women were in immediately prior to the rape, defined simply by who else was there. Women were either out alone, alone with the rapist, in a social situation, or in another situation. Of the three women who were in 'other' situations one was alone at home in bed, one was at work and one was in hospital. Social situations were broken down further (Table 3.6):

Table 3.6 Types of situation

Pre-rape situation	No.
Woman out	
alone	10
with rapist	6
In social situation	
at home	2
other home	5
public	4
Other	3

Being out alone usually meant that the women were on their way from one place to another. None of the women here had any previous contact with the men who subsequently raped them:

Diana was walking home after an evening job when a group of young men started to follow her and push her around. An older man appeared and offered to walk with her to help her out. He pulled her towards a house, suggesting she wait in his home until the others had gone away. Once inside, he began to pester her. She thought she had convinced him to leave her alone, when he opened the door and let the others in.

This offering of 'help' came up in several other situations as a useful gambit to break down mistrust and make a contact. There was something cynical in the offer of help against sexual harassment, or men assuming a very paternalistic 'concern' for the welfare of a woman alone, with comments like 'It's a dangerous part of London to be in for a young girl alone'. Two of the women were jumped from behind, the closest approximation to the common sense understanding of rape – one was on her way from work and another from school.

Where women were *alone with the rapist* there was nothing ambiguous or unusual about where they were or who they were with:

Dru had met someone at a party a few weeks before and had arranged to go out with him again.
Fiona and her husband had a 'friend of a friend' stay for a few days and, as thanks, he offered to take both of them out for a meal. Lack of baby-sitters led her husband to offer to stay behind while Fiona went for a rare night out.

Men being helpful came up again, with one friend offering to fix a washing machine, another staying behind to clear up after a party, and others offering safe lifts home. Either the relationships to the men were such that there was no reason to be worried about being alone with them, or the men had presented the situation as safe. The effect in the end was to hit hard at the trust women had in others and their own judgement. One woman summed up the confusion felt when a perfectly normal situation ends up in rape: 'What did I do to deserve this? What did I do wrong? I was nice to the bastard.'

Social situations could also lead to a shaking of confidence, if the end result was rape. In part this is because the common understanding of rape does not include innocent social gatherings and people who are known and trusted. There are sexual overtones often in public settings, because they are the situations for meeting people, including potential sexual partners, but most people believe that there are unwritten rules concerning how such contacts are made. Violence is not on most women's minds at parties, youth clubs, dinners at home and family get-togethers:

Lianne was at a party and very obviously went off with a young man in order to get her own boyfriend annoyed. Once outside the party, he turned on her and several of his friends joined in.

Sara was at a disco with friends on a weekly 'girls night out'. Two young men she had seen around the disco and seen talking to other friends offered her and a friend a lift home. As they were together, and the guys seemed OK, they thanked them and left.

Vi was having lunch with her husband when they got talking to a man who sat at their table. He got on well with both of them, and she remained to finish her coffee with him after her husband had left.

Bea was at a family 'do' when she felt ill and went to lie down. Dozing in a bedroom, she realised that her brother-in-law had come into the room.

Effy had a few friends around for a meal. One, who lived in the same block, offered to stay behind to clear up.

In dealing with the rape afterwards, certain specific responses seemed to be related to the pre-rape situation. Fear of crowds, for example, was a temporary reaction several women noted, especially if they had felt that the rape had come from a social situation (though this also could indicate a fear of being touched). Sara, for example, became very nervous in crowds for several months after the rape and said she didn't feel safe knowing that she had met her rapists in a crowd. She also was very frightened of seeing them again and scanned crowds constantly. Others commented that the sexual overtones of mixed social situations became so obvious after their experience of rape that, for some time anyway, it was painful and upsetting:

Fiona said that over dinner there had been suggestions and hints from the rapist which she had dealt with, as she always had, by making a joke of it. After the rape, she became very aggressive on first meeting people, at times mentioning the rape so that they would not make jokes or suggestions. She felt that she acted that way because the rapist had made her mistrust men and that undercurrents made her uncomfortable – she needed to know exactly what was going on.

Suggestive or explicitly sexual advertising or posters could also make women feel either upset or angry if they related their own experience to the object image of women around them. One woman, used to ignoring men's comments in the streets, just couldn't any longer. When a man passing her made a suggestive comment, she smacked him in the mouth – 'for all the times I didn't hear it before' she said.

Related to the pre-rape situation, whether or not the women knew the rapists before the attack played a significant part in how she saw what had happened to her and how she handled it. Rape by a stranger is the one we all know about, but the rapist may be known to the woman in one of several ways (Table 3.7):

Table 3.7 Prior contact with the rapist

Contact	No.
None	10
Met in pre-rape situation	5
Known through friends	8
Known personally	3
Relative	1
One known/others not (group rape)	3

For ten of the women, there was *no prior contact* with the rapists, only the assault itself. These are the situations normally seen in studies and statistics as 'stranger' rape. In these situations, the rapists either used the woman's isolation, or surprise in order to effect an assault:

Barbara was on her way home after a night out with friends when she was hit from behind.

Katy was asleep in her flat after having friends in for the evening. She woke up to find someone in her room. He said he had waited for everyone to go, then had broken in through a window.

Una was in hospital, sedated and in a room of her own. She was raped by a hospital porter.

Cathy was out walking late at night. She had a history of schizophrenia and often walked at night when there was no-one around to confuse her. A man approached her and became aggressive when she didn't answer him immediately.

In other situations, the rapist *used the pre-rape situation* to get close to or speak to the woman, and so create the potential for rape:

Pru had just arrived in a new town and was looking for somewhere to stay. An older man started talking to her, expressing concern that she was alone. She told him she needed a hotel and he said he would help her find one. He drove her to the edge of town, left her in his car, saying he needed to collect something. A group of men came out of his house and got in the car.

Rose was having a coffee after a job interview. A man began to pester her and she moved. As he persisted, she was grateful when a pleasant young man intervened and helped her get rid of him. They got talking and he seemed OK, so when he asked her out for a meal, she said yes. He was only pleasant during the meal, but turned nasty when they left the restaurant, grabbing her arm and becoming aggressive. His sudden change stunned her and prevented any effective resistance – he was also hurting her.

In these situations, the rapist is really still a stranger but one who has used one contact to mask his strangeness by acting in a friendly, helpful way.

Women were very careful to get clear how well they thought they knew the man who raped them. One category they came to was *known through friends*. This often meant that not only did the rape produce a mistrust of men, but their friends were considered as suspicious by association with the rapist, or because they introduced the woman to a man who hurt her:

Jo had been to see a friend and met a man there who she had seen around. He walked home with her, finding out that she was alone that evening. He followed her indoors. Jo couldn't get it out of her mind that the friends might have known he was dangerous.

Even worse, some women had good reason to suspect that a friend may actually have set them up for the assault:

Norma was in her boyfriend's flat waiting to go out. Another friend of his was there. Her boyfriend went out, saying he was buying cigarettes. When he went, the other man made a pass at her. When she declined to take him up on his offer, he lashed out at her. Afterwards, a thought nagged at her – how much did her boyfriend know about his friend's intentions. He didn't come back to the flat during a long assault, and made no contact with her again.

With the rapes involving more than two rapists, there also at times seemed to be an element of setting the woman up, hence the *one known/other not* which women described:

Charlotte met a friend in the street and went with him back to his house. There were usually a variety of people there, so she was not concerned when he went out and other young men came in. She started to feel nervous when she realised she was the only female and that the atmosphere wasn't friendly at all.

Women hesitated afterwards to describe a man who raped them as a friend, but some clearly were *known personally*. None of the women here had had a sexual relationship with the rapists, including the two who had been or were dating the men who raped them:

Sandy had just finished with her boyfriend but still saw him around. She thought nothing of it when he got a message to her that he wanted to see her at his home. She expected his family to be there, but they weren't.

Only one of the women was related to the man who raped her,

which was the situation where most clearly the relationship between them was defined as non-sexual. The relationship to the rapist was important in several ways. It could determine whether or not she was likely to encounter the rapist again and therefore how much she would have to take him into account in coping with the experience. If the rapist was known or not influenced how likely the woman was to turn to perhaps mutual friends for help. The prior knowledge of the rapist also made a difference to how the woman saw her experience, whether it was a breaking of trust in her feelings about people or a breaking of trust in situations.

In previous studies, rapes have at times been categorised by the relationship between the rapist and the raped women. Burgess and Holmstrom (1975), in their initial study, called stranger rapes 'blitz' attacks – literally coming out of the blue. When looking at the pre-rape situations, there is little in any of them to give any more warning than a blitz attack, at least from the woman's point of view. That the women could see after the event that the pre-rape situation involved planning and manipulation on the part of the rapist does not make her any more aware of this beforehand. When looking at the pre-rape situations, the normality, the involvement of other people and the trust we all need that those around us will not harm us, leaves the impression that, for all women, rape is always a blitz attack.

THE ASSAULT

When talking about the rape situation itself, women did not describe the exciting or thrilling experience which this society prefers to focus on, but a lonely, isolating void. In the midst of the details, feelings and reactions remained a woman trying to cope with a frightening, painful and confusing situation – a woman being victimised. Listening to women's accounts made feminism state very clearly that rape was in effect a situation where control of a woman's life was taken away from her – a truly life-threatening situation. In trying to understand what had happened to them, women brought out two other factors. The first was their perception of the attitude of the rapist, clearly relevant as the woman could only work out what was going to happen to her by concentrating on what the assailant(s) appeared to want. The second was something which took time and attention after the rape situation but which was hardly thought about at the time, and that was what she herself did or could have done in the circumstances. Being able to decide at the time how to act and why was a particular response to the experience shown by some of the women here. Whether this was possible or not, what they did during the rape did have a bearing on how they responded afterwards.

As the pre-rape situations indicated, it was not unusual for the rapist to have done a lot of groundwork. In gaining a woman's   trust   or   using   a relationship to create opportunity, not all the rapists needed to strike suddenly or be waiting and hiding, nor did they necessarily need to use more violence than the rape itself. What was required of them was the intention to inflict harm.

Moving from the pre-rape situation to the assault itself sometimes required moving from one place to another, and sometimes only required other people to move (Table 3.8). The physical shifting from one situation to another was not necessarily any more of a warning of the assault than any other behaviour or action on the part of the rapists had been. For the women, the assault started at the point they realised something was wrong.

Table 3.8 Getting into the assault situation

Getting there	No.
Went with rapist (voluntary)	11
Taken by rapist (forced)	4
Sudden attack when alone	7
Left pre-rape situation alone	5
Stayed in same place with rapist	3
Assault setting	
Outside	
country	6
town	6
Rapist's home	5
Own home	5
Other home	4
Other	4*

* 1 in hospital, 1 at work, 1 repeat assaults/different places, 1 not known clearly.

Alice was with her friend's father who was helping her to buy something for the flat. As they had to wait for the order to be made up, he suggested a walk in nearby park-land, to pass the time. She thought nothing of it, until they turned into a wooded area and seemed to be going too far for a short walk. She was more worried about being lost (because he remained just friendly) than thinking he may be intentionally isolating her, until he suddenly grabbed at her and pushed her down. She was so stunned she hardly struggled.

Iris was offered a lift at a bus stop. She felt OK with the two men in the car at first but asked to get out when she realised that the driver had been drinking. She was more annoyed than worried at that point.

Gemma was working late in public offices, when a gang of young men walked in. She ordered them out but then saw that one of them had a knife.

Some of the women commented about sudden changes in behaviour or attitude as being the most frightening thing about the start of the assault. Others went repeatedly over the first steps – going for the walk, getting into the car, trying to find some missed hint that would have warned them, if they had seen it at the time. For all the women who were conscious, the switch from a seemingly normal situation to rape was instantaneous, and the shock of the sudden revelation of the assault was as effective at immobilising them as a blow on the head was for others.

The details of the assault were important for the woman who had suffered it (Table 3.9), and being able to talk about the details

Table 3.9 Number of assaults and types of assault

Number of assailants	No. of women assaulted
One	21
Two	2
Three	3
More than three	4

Types of assault	No. of women assaulted
Vaginal rape by penis	30
Oral rape by penis	5
Anal rape by penis	4
Beaten up	10
Stabbed	2
Other	2

can be a way of dealing with the assault and putting it in the past. There was no other clear connection, however, with such factors as the amount of violence used or types of sexual abuse and later coping or response. More important was why it had been done to them and the expressed attitude of the rapists (Table 3.10).

Table 3.10 Perceived attitudes of the rapists

Woman's perception	No.
Woman passed out/no interaction	3
'This isn't rape really'	4
'What a joke'	6
Anger aimed at woman personally	9
General anger	4
Power/control	2
Matter of fact	2

Yvonne made the point clearly. She was badly beaten during the rape and the physical assault was brutal. What tormented her afterwards was not what he had done, but why. 'This doesn't matter' she said, pointing to a swollen lip, 'but that man fucked my mind.'
Enid was knocked out and had no idea who the rapist(s) were or what they did.

Several of the women *passed out* at some point during the assault, and one other was knocked out from the start. When noticed, the attitude of the rapists really got through to the women:

Effy was at first confused, but then became furious when she explained that, during the rape, the rapist had complained about her lying too still and not trying to enjoy it or help him to enjoy it more. This was despite the fact that she had struggled, and he had had to knock her down in order to be able to rape her. Afterwards he sulked that she had spoilt it for him.

In trying to find an explanation for this kind of denial of rape (seen by the woman as the rapist saying *'This isn't rape, you know'*), some women thought that there was a deliberate attempt to confuse them, to silence them afterwards or to make them less willing to tell anyone. Each woman felt it was a negation of their feelings and added to the humiliation. They felt more out of control as a result; not only was the rapist capable of raping them but he also wanted to control the definition of it as well.

In some situations, the rapists clearly knew that what they were doing was rape but thought the whole thing *a laugh*. This was especially true where more than one rapist was involved and where the rape was used as amusement for the group. Women felt that the laughing, taunting and added humiliations were part of the whole assault, that it acted as 'an extra' for the rapists that they were able to make their friends laugh and the increased humiliation of the woman added to their feelings of power and control. In one situation where one rapist was involved, he seemed to be smiling at a private joke throughout. As he left, he turned and said 'don't get raped'.

In some situations, the women said that they felt it could have been any woman it was being done to, that they as individuals didn't count. Only where the rapists seemed *angry at the woman personally* did those women feel that the rape had been also aimed only at them:

Fiona was walking with the rapist when he said he needed something from the car and went back. He had not given any hint that he was upset or angry at her. As she walked, he suddenly grabbed her from behind and pushed her into nearby fields. He beat her while he pulled at her clothes, but his temper itself was quite overpowering. She said he seemed furious. During the rape he said she was getting what was coming to her and 'it's only what you really wanted anyway'.

Where anger was so clear, the women all had had some previous contact with the rapist and the anger did seem to be built up around some perceived slight, perceived by the women only afterwards and with a thorough review of all and any contact with him.

This focused anger contrasted with the feeling other women had that the *anger* shown by the rapists was *not aimed at them* but that they had somehow got in the way of it. Terri, for example, felt that any woman pulled off the street would have been used to work off her rapist's anger and frustration.

Four of the women here found it hard to describe at first what the attitude of their rapists was because it seemed more complex than a straightforward emotion or aim. Two of the women felt that the whole assault was concerned with *power and control* so that even sexual feelings were subsumed under that as far as the rapists were concerned:

Rose began to feel she would never get away from the rapist and would always be at risk from him. He raped her first at what may have been his own home but could have belonged to someone he knew. She got away and found her way home, but he had taken things out of her bag which gave him her name and phone number. He phoned, terrorising her, then turned up and forced his way in. He alternated between being friendly if anyone was around and totally threatening, constantly getting at her, when they were alone. He said he was going to make her work for him, on the streets and that she would do it, whatever she thought. She felt overwhelmed and resigned herself to death. Only telling someone what was happening finally broke the spell.

Finally, two women commented that the rapists appeared very *matter-of-fact* and seemed to feel just that it was a job to be done. Both also said that their own reaction was to cut themselves off from what was happening, to shut down their awareness, so were less perceptive to what the rapist was showing of his own feelings. They were both raped by men who were found to be repeat offenders and may have been disturbed to the extent that the rape was an unemotional thing for them.

Trying to assess and judge the rapist was the one way that women maintained some level of control in a situation where the potential to change the situation or end it was limited; although out of control of the rape, women could at least observe and be ready for escape or for coping afterwards. Their own reactions during the assault were part instinctive and partly considered (Table 3.11).

Table 3.11 Women's reactions during the assault

Reaction	No.
No struggle	
immobilised	14
maintained calm front	2
Struggled/fought back	14

When rape was first taken up as a 'social problem', one response was an outpouring of advice on how to behave during a rape attack. Some so-called self-defence experts made a lot of money writing books and touring campuses in the US, advising women not to fight back, to try to talk their way out of it but otherwise to let the rapist get on with it. Such advice assumed a level of control which women, then and now, were saying 'we don't have'. The usual advice from the police was not to fight back because doing so could increase injuries (and this, according to studies, has some truth in it) yet women knew that only evidence of total struggle convinced a judge and jury that rape took place. The main statement from the Women's Movement, for the organisations listening to raped women, was 'you can only do what you can do at the time'.

For the women here who said they could only describe their reaction as *immobilised*, what they could do was a lot different from what they wanted to do, or what they thought of doing afterwards:

Charlotte was immobilised by sheer numbers. She had no idea how many men were in the room when the one she knew left, but between eight and ten. At first, she struggled with the idea that someone she knew, who she liked, could possibly set her up for such an assault. Once she did see what was happening, she knew she couldn't fight her way out of it.

The fear generated by a gang, or a gang and a knife as in Gemma's case, prevented thoughts of anything but staying alive. Others also talked of the confusion and shock of realising that rape was happening and the feeling of being stunned into total passivity, as for Bea where she had first to acknowledge that her brother-in-law was there and intending to rape her. It was not, she said, that she decided not to call out or make a fuss and alert others in the house, but that she didn't believe what was happening and couldn't think once the reality had sunk in. For others, the realisation was followed immediately by the threat or use of violence which prevented any action:

Norma was swung from a normal situation containing no threat into a violent chaos with one slap from the rapist. The assault continued with pain so intense at times that she passed out. He did not need to hurt her as much as he did, as she was a very nervous woman who tended to look to men for protection. She was immobilised by the first blow and the rest was for his benefit entirely.

Some women began by struggling but stopped as soon as violence or the threat of it was used:

Vi, lulled by his friendly manner into the rapist's home, did try to talk her way out of it when she first realised that he intended to harm her. He had locked her in and said she would have to stay there and no-one knew where she was. She therefore had both the immediate threat of rape, which he said was his intention, and the belief that the situation would last a long time. She shouted at him and his reaction was to get angry in return. Although at the time fear silenced her, she saw afterwards that only by withdrawing did she have any chance of being prepared for escape if the opportunity came.

Drugs or drink certainly inhibit reactions in two situations:

Zoe had been at a party and had been drinking more than she could cope with. She went to lie down when she felt ill, thinking she would wait a while before going home. She sensed someone had come into the room but couldn't stop him when he raped her. She said the worst part was the feeling of being unable to get through her sickness and drunken feeling to even understand what was happening.

For two of the women, the reaction was considered, and was a *maintained calm*. Although very frightened, they had made themselves stay calm and passive, to help them get through:

Diana accepted that she couldn't fight her way out of a rape situation which included upwards of ten rapists. She had some time to think through her situation and decided, whatever they did, not to show her fear or upset. They laughed at her and tried to provoke her but she maintained what she called 'integrity'. It was important to her afterwards that they had not beaten her mentally, whatever else they did.
Hilda also forced herself to remain calm though with no clear idea why at the time. The rapist said he had a knife and she had no reason to doubt him. She thought that by showing the least possible opposition, he would be less tempted to use the knife and she would have more of a chance to get away.

Fear and anger were the prevailing emotions in the women during the assault itself – in varying combinations and amounts. If anger surfaced in the early stages of the assault, it did sometimes fuel a determination to *fight back*:

Dru, once over the shock of having a seemingly nice 'date' turn nasty, became angry at him. He had hurt her dragging her into a derelict shed and she had no illusions that she would actually fight him off, but she continued to struggle as much as she could, saying afterwards 'I didn't want him to have any illusions that it wasn't rape.'
Wanda was held down by several young men while they tried to rape her. She refused to give in without a fight, angry at being picked out for such an assault. She felt some consolation afterwards that she had prevented two of the gang penetrating her, so had not been an 'easy mark'.

Other women struggled more out of fear than anger:

Anni kept up a struggle hoping that the rapist would see what he was doing and stop. She got the feeling that he used just enough force to combat her resistance and would have hurt her more if he had to. She also thought that he was being careful not to leave marks as he commented on that and how no-one would believe her that she had been raped – she'd let him in, stayed alone with him and he hadn't hurt her.

Such rational attacks were both frightening and hard to fight against.

In each of the women's reactions during the assault there were elements of decision-making as well as instinctive or unthinking behaviour. Some women managed to distance themselves from the assault even when it was happening, while others were distanced by shock, pain or blows. By watching the rapists and judging their attitudes, they decided what the situation meant for themselves. What happened during the rape itself, in terms of understanding the rapist's and the woman's own reactions, was followed through in the process of victimisation by how the women coped later. How the rape situation ended (Table 3.12) was both the start of the post-rape situation and had an influence on what happened in that first few hours afterwards.

Table 3.12 Ending the rape situation

Rapist exits	No.
With threats	8
Unconcerned	6
Being friendly	3
Ran (disturbed)	1

Woman exits	No.
Allowed to go	
with threats	2
rapist unconcerned	2
Came-to alone	2
Escaped	6

Threats from the rapist was one particular exit which caused disturbance for the women, especially just after the rape, because threats potentially extended the rape situation into the future, or left the chance that it could happen again. Where threats were used and the rapist left or allowed the woman to leave, the rapist remained in control right to the end:

Sandy got to the door when the rapist told her not to tell anyone or he would 'get' her father. She was very young and believed he meant the threat. He also knew her family and mentioned opportunities he would have of carrying the threat out. She had to believe him and told no-one until months later her mother realised she was pregnant. Even then, she would not immediately tell anyone what had happened, only blurting it out when her mother said she would ask her sister who Sandy had been seen around with. Despite reassurances, she remained at least uncertain about whether he could carry out the threat.

Threats against people close to the woman, rather than directly against her, were the more common, as if acknowledging women's primary social role as carers. Women had to consider threats to their children, partners, younger sister or parents, making who to tell and how to respond take on an extra dimension and making support always tinged with concern.

When the rapists left, or allowed the woman to leave, *unconcerned*, women expressed a mixture of shame and confusion. They felt it as a dismissal, as if they had been objects now discarded. Such a response also suggested a sense of arrogance on the part of the rapists, a sureness that they would get away with it:

Pru said that the rapists seemed to have forgotten she was there as she scrambled away. They were sitting around talking and didn't acknowledge she was going.
Effy was left lying on the floor and her rapist muttered 'see you around' on his way out. She said 'I don't know what I expected to happen – an apology, a threat, something that would have said to me, at least he knows what he's done. That comment made me more alone than anything else.'

Such feelings were also associated with the situations where the rapists maintained a jokey or *friendly* attitude to the bitter end. By sticking to the intepretation of the rape as 'not rape', the meaning remained obscure. There was also an implied threat – if they really didn't see what was wrong with what they'd done, perhaps they'd try again.

For some of the women, the rape ended as abruptly as it began. Lianne's rapists were disturbed by the police and she was thrown straight from the rape into another fraught situation out of her control. Enid and Barbara were both left in the street unconscious. Only those women who got out of the situation for themselves had any sense of ending the rape under their own control, of *escaping*. Each had to, in fact, wait for some break in the rapist's attention and until the rapist had to some extent finished with them:

Yvonne had tried to get away throughout the rape, but only got her real opportunity when the rapist fell asleep. She crept out and then ran – almost under the wheels of a taxi, the driver of which called the police and took her straight to hospital. Asked by the police why she hadn't got away before she replied: 'I don't usually think too well when I'm scared and being beaten up. Ask me that stupid question again when you've been raped.'

In these various ways, the women came through the rape situation and into the part of the process where they had to start dealing with it as a part of their lives. Through the pre-rape situation, the women were in ignorance of what was going to happen and sometimes the rapist was actively manipulating the situation and her to ensure that rape would take place. During the rape itself, the rapists took control of the situation, leaving women only able to work with their understanding of what was happening and their own reactions. Once the act of rape was over, the rapist had only to get out of the situation but the women had to begin to cope. The next step was marked by decisions which needed to be made – at a time when such decisions would be harder than usual. The issue of control remained right through coping but especially in the immediate aftermath, when involving others could mean that the women still felt out of control.

THE POST-RAPE SITUATION

Where to go and who to tell were the two most urgent questions the women had to answer for themselves once they could feel that the immediate assault was over. Behind both questions was a third – why? From the act of rape ending, women were making decisions about how best to deal with their own victimisation. When talking afterwards about this immediate post-rape time women were very clear about the difference between things they had done for a purpose and those they had had no choice over.

The first move (Table 3.13) was either to go somewhere that the women felt was safe, or where they thought they ought to go, or where they had no choice but to go. If they had been raped

Table 3.13 The first move

Moved to	No.
Own home	13
Others' home	4
Hospital	4
Police	5
Stayed where rape occurred	4

away from their own homes, then *going home* was an obvious
first move. Sara headed for home because it represented
safety and an end to the assault, Terri had a child she had to get
back to, while Enid went home without thinking. Olivia drag-
ged herself to a friend's house because she needed both help and
company, and Charlotte headed not really for a place but for her
mother.

Going to hospital as a first step wasn't usually a choice at all
but was decided by others because of the injuries the women had
received. Iris was taken there by the police as was Pru, both
unable to have a say in it and not sure where they were or who
they were with.

There was an element of choice about going straight to the
police, though the reasoning behind the choice varied. Norma
was found in the street by a policeman, while Vi, having escaped
from a virtual prison, was angry and wanted immediate action.
Wanda and Jo both felt they ought to, though Wanda didn't like
the idea. Jo believed they would help her. None of the women
who went straight to the police felt they had got sympathetic
treatment and Jo, who had most faith in what the police would
be like, was horrified at their off-hand reaction.

Those who *stayed* where the rape had happened, were either
in their own homes or, for Una, in hospital and unable to go any-
where. Although frightened and insecure in homes that had
been violated, the women still felt less frightened about staying
where they were than going outside.

As with the first move, who to tell and why was sometimes a
choice and sometimes out of their hands. Injury was one factor
which often meant that more people were involved than the
women would have wanted, but even injuries were hidden by
some who were determined to hide the rape, for whatever

reason. Who else was told and why had important repercussions for dealing with the total process because it again represented control. Choice meant more chance of getting the necessary support without handing over control to others. When choice was removed, the women felt more vulnerable and the post-rape situation was extended while they struggled to regain control. Only someone who has faced the situation of having someone else forcibly take over their lives can understand the true relevance that control had in the assault and in the first few hours afterwards.

Some women involved only the immediate family or partner, very clearly sharing their experience with a trusted other:

Anni waited until her husband got home from work and immediately poured the whole story out to him, feeling that it was then their problem and not hers. Together they decided not to go to the police, because that could upset Anni more and still not deal with the rapist, but to get in touch with the RCC for extra support for her. The focus during this time was very much on support and care for Anni as someone who had been hurt. Only later did the injustice of it come through.

Katy waited until daylight then left her flat and ran to her mother. Together they decided to go to a doctor and the police – people Katy could not handle on her own but felt she ought to involve. She managed it, with her mother.

Others would have preferred in some ways not to involve anyone, but they realised early on that they would not cope without help. One woman remarked that not telling anyone might have made it easier to pretend nothing had happened – but something had:

Barbara was hurt and knew she would need treatment apart from anything else. She also knew that keeping quiet about the rape would be an impossible burden. She found her way home and, after several drinks, told her flatmates. With their help, she contacted the police and went to hospital. She didn't feel she could share the experience exactly but at least others knew what had happened.

The response of others at this time was vital and a negative response very hard for the women to take. As with Jo, who was faced with total apathy from the police, a negative response from whoever was told first made it difficult for them seek support or help elsewhere. Diana had friends who were very supportive but allowed her to stay in control, and parents who alternated between hysteria and taking over. She had a clear idea which she found most useful. Iris was scared because she found the staff uncaring and could hear an argument going on somewhere. She registered only that, instead of safety and care, she heard aggression still surrounding her. Patience was told off by her parents who at first didn't believe her and then questioned her about why she was in a park she had been told not to go in. Such responses, because they are out of the woman's control and because they go against everything she needs, can effectively silence raped women for years, until they can find the trust that someone else will not ignore them or blame them for what had happened.

The first few days following the rape itself was the time when the physical after-effects were most noticable (except for pregnancy when the fear of it could dominate instead). Many of the women reported nightmares, sleep disturbances, headaches, other aches, vomiting, shivering and other physical effects of shock or trauma. Five of the women had injuries which required treatment. Such reactions, which did seem to be out of their control, tended to extend the period of time where the women felt the rape was with them. The reactions also had to be coped with as part of the whole process of victimisation. Two ways of responding, in this post-rape time, were noted.

For some women, what followed the rape was a period of time which was still out of their control, but relatively safe. In this case, the feeling was usually associated with the involvement of others outside the woman's control anyway. Women saw that in this time they were either saying 'Take over, I can't cope' or they saw that they were not in a position to cope for themselves, because others were blocking it:

Yvonne panicked at the hospital and became hysterical. No-one knew at the time that the rapist had given her drugs which, although she was used to them, confused her further. Once out of that situation, though, she got hold of other drugs and, with drink also, and hardly any sleep, stayed blasted for days. She stumbled on in a terrified haze, allowing others around her to organise things and at the same time fearful that they would harm her further. She acknowledged later that it was not an unusual response of hers to disturbance.

To an observer, there could be little difference between the *un-controlled* reaction of someone like Yvonne and the *controlled release of feeling described by others. Una knew that blocking* her feelings would harm her more so let them out. She screamed, cried and shook, but 'allowed herself to' rather than letting the reactions themselves take over. Diana also let her feelings out with her friends, but hid them quickly when her mother really went out of control on hearing about the rape.

A third type of response women here showed was *hidden*. Some women held their feelings down to hide the rape from others or because they were afraid of their own emotions, while some, such as Iris, found that others effectively blocked any expression of feeling at all. Sara hid her response at first, to keep it from her family and to sort out her feelings for herself. Enid's response was to withdraw to the extent that her depression was not concealed, but obvious. Hilda wanted time to think about what she should do so kept her feelings in while she did so.

Whether uncontrolled, controlled, or hidden, the immediate response did not necessarily show how women would cope in the longer term. In a way, the post-rape situation was dealing with the act of rape alone. Coping with the process of victimisation, once the rape itself was moving into the past, included so much else that the post-rape responses became in effect another thing to cope with.

4 RESPONDING TO VICTIMISATION THROUGH RAPE

and i have had to live with it
to deal with it (oh and i do mean that literally
oh so literally)
deal with it
everyday at least one

so i've done the best i can
with words with poetry
the voice of my honesty
i have tried to create something positive
out of nightmare lessons

(extract from 'a letter to you my sisters',
poem by dell fitzgerald-richards,
published by Women's Press Collective,
Oakland, CA, USA, n.d.)

The immediate post-rape situation reflects most clearly what we understand as victimisation and being a victim. In the short term after an assault, women may show physical signs and will be expected to show some kind of emotional response. Time for those around a woman who has been raped may then get out of synchrony with hers, as the rape for them becomes history. For her, she is starting to learn to live with it, but other situations and incidents enter into her life, creating new issues to deal with, and keeping the rape in the present. What emerges from how a woman copes with the whole process of victimisation is an image of the kind of 'victim' she sees herself as, what she believes has happened to her, and therefore what choices she makes to come through the experience as a person. The accounts of these thirty women showed no single, identifiable 'victim' status, no blueprint for how a woman who is raped does or does not act. What the women shared in their accounts was how they understood what had happened to them, drawing on their experience of rape and reactions, their own lives, those around them and the political or social image of rape and victimisation. Taken together, the women showed a range of types of victimisation, just as they had also described a range of rape experiences.

In this study, the shortest period of time from the rape to the end of contact with a woman was six months, and the longest time sixteen years. For the majority of the thirty women, there was information on at least one year of their lives after a rape assault. As the length of time from the rape increased, it was more likely that other factors in a woman's situation would begin to affect how she was feeling and how she saw herself. One thing which became clear was that women often felt that a time had come when they were no longer 'victims' but 'recovered'. Women who have been raped, and researchers and counsellors all seem to have an understanding of victimisation as a process, situation or condition (depending on outlook), with an end.

In looking at coping, the first stage was to examine the elements of women's lives which might show the response to victimisation, and which may also indicate differences in understanding or perception on the part of the women. A final three elements, one from each level of the process (personal, interpersonal and social), were drawn out from the accounts and information because they showed an understanding of the whole process.

Sexuality, as a personal element of women's lives, showed an understanding of the rape experience as well as allowing the woman to express something about her own self-image. Sexual and other close relationships and the effect on them of the rape experience was the element on the interpersonal level chosen because it was through relationships that women could express how they felt about the immediate world around them. This linked the personal level with the public, connecting with changes in social life following rape, because it showed the public identity, how women saw themselves in the world.

Together, the three elements allowed a picture to be built up which expressed the type of victimisation the women felt they had suffered, and how they intended dealing with it.

SELF-IMAGE, SEXUAL EXPRESSION AND THE
EXPERIENCE OF RAPE

When talking about their sexual experiences or feelings after rape, the women in this study really talked about two distinct but related feelings. Firstly, they talked about their feelings about their own bodies. A woman who felt her body had been changed, damaged or permanently degraded by the rape would find it difficult to believe that anyone else would approach her with anything other than disgust or to hurt her again. On the other hand, a woman who could feel that the rape had affected her as an accident (that she was hurt but it would get better) would eventually accept that her attractiveness and sexuality were innocent and unconnected with rape:

Enid showed an extreme response to her own body, going from a very smart and carefully dressed young woman to someone who looked untidy and uncared for (except that her skin was sore from continual scrubbing) three months after the rape. She was pregnant as a result of the rape, and referred to the pregnancy as the 'parasite they left behind'. She couldn't understand why her family and friends still cared for her, because she couldn't care for herself. Care for her appearance, she said, had been a reflection of her self-assurance and confidence in her life. After the rape, she pulled at herself, hid behind strands of hair, and laughed cynically at the idea that she could ever become again a person who others would respect, because she had lost self-respect.
Sara was horrified at the filth which surrounded her when she was raped, and the smell of the rapists, but had cleared herself from it once she bathed and it was physically gone. She had a confidence in her own attractiveness as a person and never felt damaged or changed by the rape.

In looking at what women felt about their bodies, it was clearly no coincidence for some that they hurt or damaged themselves in the first few months after the rape. Sometimes it was clearly deliberate:

Yvonne was covered in scars before the rape and several were added afterwards, when confusion and anger took over and she had no-one else to hurt but herself. Between gashes on her wrists, overdoses, setting fire to herself and 'falling' down stairs, Yvonne showed an extreme desire for self-destruction. When talking about her feelings when she hurt herself, she would say that sometimes she felt angry and, given other people had taken their anger out on her, she supposed she did the same. Sometimes, it was a desire not to have to face the psychic pain of victimisation and so there were real attempts to die. Sometimes it was sheer confusion.

With others, there were accidents, sometimes associated with drink or tranquillisers. They were taken to deaden the feelings, but also made them clumsy:

Fiona, in the first year after the rape, suffered a number of minor injuries. Otherwise, she always looked well dressed and smart. The injuries always appeared to be accidental, but tended to occur when she had been drinking, or when she was upset or depressed. One result of the injuries was to focus her own and others' attention on her pain, a focus she found easier to elicit from her family and friends for physical hurt rather than her emotional pain of the rape. Her family were closed up, unable or unwilling to show support. The injuries, she recognised, were a physical symbol of her victimisation and gave her the attention and support she needed. She was central to the situation and because she caused the injuries, she was in control.

Where a negative self-image was clearly operating for the women, it was associated with depression, where others were not involved or were not giving support, or where feelings were suppressed at the start. Where a good self-image was maintained, the women were able to express their anger at others, had good support and could feel that others saw them still as whole people, not just as victims or damaged goods.

The second way that women expressed their understanding of the rape was in their response to sexual activity. Some of the women were in sexual relationships at the time of the rape, others had to look at sex when they met a new partner; some of the women deliberately had sex with someone to find out how they felt:

Bea was happily married with a supportive and mutually satisfactory sexual relationship. When she was raped by her brother-in-law, her husband was concerned not to do anything wrong. He didn't want to feel he was pressuring her into sex too early after the experience, but equally didn't want her to think he no longer found her attractive. Luckily, Bea had never felt reticent about letting him know how she felt about sexual activity, so was able to reassure him that she would let him know when she was ready. It was about six months after the rape before they finally settled back into an easy relationship again, but physical comfort had been maintained between them, and she had found his concern the most positive response possible.

Patience had been raped in her early teens and felt that the experience had affected her eventual sexual relationship with her husband. She disliked intercourse but wanted physical affection. She had seen a therapist who had dismissed the rape as irrelevant and left her feeling she was inadequate because she was selfish and not thinking of her husband. (Her parents had told her to 'think about others' when they blamed her for causing a fuss about the rape.) Her husband didn't see sex was anything without intercourse, wanted her 'better' and resented the idea that she associated anything he did with the rape. She said she knew that the rape was only a part of the problem, but that she needed to sort it out and have it accepted as important.

Pru returned home as soon as she was released from hospital. She decided not to tell anyone when she got home, because she wanted to get over it quicker. This worked for her in most areas of her life – except sex. The relationship she was involved in at the time of the rape ended soon after her return, she felt partly because of her lack of responsiveness. Two years after the rape, she still felt cold sexually, only going through the motions for the sake of her partner and for the physical affection. Pru felt that she feared being out of control in sexual situations, and the only control she had was over her own (lack of) feelings. She had never told a sexual partner about the rape, because she had never trusted a man with that information. She was still angry about her experience, and could express this easily to the RCC and, eventually, in therapy. She saw that not involving others had blocked ways of expressing and getting out her feelings, which was most clearly shown in her sexual expression.

Several of the women either contacted the RCC soon after attempting sexual activity, or called in distress because sex had made them feel in a crisis once more. Often, the sexual activity had been approached with an idea of finding out how it would feel, as for Zoe, who wanted to know if she could find sex a pleasure again after the rape. It was possible also that the rape experience changed the attitudes towards sexual relationships which women had held beforehand:

Hilda had good support and never saw the rape as a personal attack. She felt that it could have been any woman who was jumped by her attacker and she was unlucky. She had good support, remained very much in control of what happened to her during the first few months and seemed able to work through issues and feelings as they arose. She was not in a relationship at the time of the rape, and did not get involved with anyone sexually for well over a year. She remarked, about two years after the rape, that she had started to see the relationships she had been involved with before as akin to rape in some ways, where men she had been involved in would be at least unconcerned about her will or feelings. She felt she could never allow herself to be treated so inhumanly again.

In this group, half were involved in some kind of steady relationship at the time of the rape, and half of those split with that partner within a year of the rape. Some of the partners were unable to cope with the idea of rape – perhaps not believing, perhaps facing a kind of jealousy. In some situations, it was the woman's response to the rape which partners found difficult to handle. Both male and female lovers at times could not understand why the rape would affect their loving relationship, not seeing the effect that negative feelings about her own body could have on a woman's sexual responses. If you believe yourself to be dirty or ugly, it is very hard to accept that someone else doesn't see it that way:

Barbara found her lover irritated that a heterosexual rape was interfering with their lesbian relationship, but Barbara felt she had been raped because she was a lesbian, and took that as a very personal hurt.

Where a relationship survived, the partners had been able to share, in some way, the total experience of victimisation and were able to give and take support. Alice's girlfriend could handle the effect rape had had, and made it clear that coping meant together. Some of the relationships which 'survived' had added problems, as with Gemma, who couldn't tell her husband about the rape she suffered and couldn't ever say no to him. She hadn't enjoyed sex before the rape and hated it afterwards, but felt that her husband's sexual selfishness trapped her into 'giving in' for the sake of peace. One woman, not in this sample, in fact never having called her own experience rape, made clear her understanding that her body was not her own to use through her one sad and self-hurting rebellion. Asked why she didn't use contraception, though did not want to get pregnant, she said 'why should I use something when sex is what he wants? I don't want to do it, I won't make it possible.' There was no other protest in her power to make.

It was impossible to view a woman's understanding of her experience of rape through her sexual identity without seeing her in the context of a wider social life. For some of the women, rape had occurred in social situations where sex could, quite harmlessly, be present. Some of the women were lonely or isolated and relied on sexual relationships for their social life. Others had been in situations where the rapists had used a non-sexual trust to be able to commit the assault. It was not surprising then, that women also found that they were looking at their social lives in responding to rape – and sometimes finding problems.

DEALING WITH RAPE IN A SOCIAL SETTING

The situations these women were in immediately before they had been raped show how such victimisation cannot be separated out from normal social life. Neither can the process of response which women go through afterwards. A study, in South Carolina, of 165 women who had been raped, made the following comment about social and leisure activities:

> Social and leisure activities were also disrupted for the first two months following the rape. Some of the items in this sub-scale concern frequency of spare time activities that may be curtailed for some time out of fear, and several other questions concerning friendships, such as arguments with friends, being hurt or offended by friends, or being lonely and uncomfortable with friends. The differences between the two groups (CONTROL and 'VICTIM') indicate that during the two months following the assault, the victims and their friends may be having difficulties relating to one another, either because of the friends' discomfort or the victim's sensitivity and changed needs in the relationship.
>
> (Resick et al., 1981, p. 711)

Three of the women in this study lost their jobs shortly after the rape and remained unemployed for several months. The loss of the job was clearly related for the women to the rape, either because they were in insecure positions and their need for time off or the disruption had been used as an excuse to get rid of them, or their distress made it impossible to continue. Their continued unemployment was in part due to the general level of unemployment, but equally looking for a new job was a big step at a time when they found it difficult to do more than exist. Two other women reported difficulties within their working environment, mainly the strain of covering up, but others reported little or no disruption. In some situations, the support of others at work turned the holding down of the job into the focus for stability and normality and helped the women to put the experience of rape behind them: being a worker was a more positive status than being a victim.

For the women who were unemployed, or at home full-time with children, there was at times an added isolation they imposed on themselves after the rape. Fiona, for example, could not continue to see the friends she knew who also knew the rapist, feeling that they had, by still seeing him, chosen who to believe. Lianne also knew her attackers and had the added anger of knowing that word would have gone around the neighbourhood that she was 'easy game', just as she knew she had been targeted in the rape for regular male entertainment. She saw her change in social life not so much as a restriction but as a learning to be self reliant; she withdrew to ensure that she would not be used again.

Norma relied totally on male company for her social life, which revolved around local pubs and one group of people. She felt they all were on the side of the rapist and her ex-boyfriend, who she suspected of at least allowing the rape to happen. She couldn't go to pubs alone because she felt conspicuous and vulnerable, and knew well enough what men thought of women who drank alone in pubs. Loneliness had been a major issue in her life before the rape, masked by her dependence on men, but, once the prop was removed by the rape, her response to victimisation really centred on her isolation and low self-esteem. Eventually, and only once the court case was over, she started going to evening classes and dancing classes, which gave her mixed company which did not focus on her as a woman looking for a man.

Anni also shared her circle of friends with her rapist and was upset at what he might be saying about her. Unlike Norma though, she had good support and enough self-confidence to believe in herself and expect others to do the same. At first she found herself not wanting to see others or go places he might be, but they lived in a small town and it was impossible without locking themselves in. Finally, Anni and her husband decided to block things for him and leave their social situation clear for her. Their social life centred on a club where the rapist was also a member. Their response was to report the rape to the committee and have him barred.

When Anni decided on this course of action, I really doubted the sanity of it, in case the very conservative community chose not to accept her accounts or needs. The effect of such a blow to her self-esteem could have been disastrous. Luckily, the club and their friends backed her and her husband to the hilt; she was vindicated and left secure in her social life. (I was thankful I had kept my doubts to myself and see now the coward in me.)

For some of the women, their social life was a strengthening part of their response. Sara's friends, for example, saw it as their job to ensure that the rapists did not restrict or stop her enjoyment of life. The only adjustment was that she went out more with her boyfriend than she did before, which could have happened anyway as part of the development of their relationship. Diana also commented that at times she made herself go out to prove that she was OK, and her friends supported her. The level and quality of support from others was crucial in this element of response, because how a woman felt about her social situation was a reflection of how she saw herself through others' eyes – it was the public face of victimisation.

There was a more personal level of response which affected social life and adjustment, but which also indicated the woman's understanding of her situation and self-image. Twelve of the women in this study showed symptoms of depression up to at least six months after the rape, and seven of them received in-patient treatment. Depression could be a much longer-term problem if crisis points in the process of victimisation served to disturb the balance women were trying hard to maintain.

HANDLING DEPRESSION

There were a variety of responses which were considered to be an indication of depression: suicide attempts, anxiety, lethargy, sleep disturbance, withdrawal, low self-esteem. In this and other studies, depression can be seen both as a response to feeling out of control, and as anger turned inwards. Women expressed depression as feeling that nothing could change how bad they felt, or nothing would change in their lives, or nothing could change what had happened to them.

In one study, depression was noted within four months of the rape. This study also stressed that details of the attack, and the severity, was not an indication of depression, but the woman's overall situation and the response of friends and family are both important (see Atkeson *et al.*, 1982, p. 101).

When women talked about depression here, it was also clear that the situation and others around influenced response. What was also noted was that hidden reactions during the post-rape situation and in the first few weeks, could delay the onset of depression, if this was going to be a factor. Women tended towards depression where they had little support, where others made their victimisation worse for them, where their response in other situations had included depression, and where they believed that the rape was aimed at them personally.

Barbara, within a few weeks of the rape, had her lover walk out on her, lost her job, had painful injuries, was pregnant and had an abortion. She tried to commit suicide, really saying 'enough is enough'. She became withdrawn, mistrustful and aimless for several months, until the friends who did support her managed to convince her she could start again. Barbara also felt that she had been picked on personally.

There were various reasons women thought that a rapist had 'chosen' them specifically:

Rose and **Iris** had both been made to feel lacking by their families – Rose's brother commented that 'she brought all this on herself and the rest of us' (this was his response to her suicide attempt). Both began to feel, after the rape, that there was something about them that the rapists had seen, which encouraged the attack, perhaps even that they could 'make' people do bad things. For both, also, the rapists had seemed so powerful that they believed that they could still be hurt by them. In some ways, the only way they could feel any security or control over their lives was to believe they had started it all, and that by hiding or withdrawing they could stop it. It was a very destructive security though.

Where women managed to avoid depression, they usually had good support from friends or family, and considered the rape as accidental or at least, something which could have happened to any woman. They were also more able to express anger and distress towards the rapists and others from the start, so distanced themselves from responsibility for the rape as well as having an outlet for feelings:

Wanda fought all the way through the rape and had to keep on fighting afterwards. She was angry at the boys who assaulted her. She was crying and shaking talking to her family and the police, but was determined that the rape would not break her. No-one blocked her anger, though her mother seemed to resent the trouble she was causing, and the police were hostile to her because she wasn't behaving like a 'real' victim. Her friends and family helped her to avoid self-blame and to use her anger – to not be a 'real victim', in effect. Several weeks after the attack, she cornered one of the boys who had raped her and scared him badly. That pleased her.

From looking at depression, the next step was clearly to examine the differences the women felt there was between rape as a personal or impersonal attack.

LOOKING AT RAPE AS A PERSONAL OR IMPERSONAL ATTACK

The distinction between a personal and impersonal attack is a lot clearer on paper than it ever was or is in reality. It is the difficulty of classifications that they have clear edges, acting as snapshots which give a taste of what was seen but never the full picture. The advantage of using classifications is that attention is focused on a useful path or insight – we do, after all, only aim the camera at what interests us. In beginning now to categorise responses, the aim is to present an image of victimisation from the point of view of the women who experienced it, through explaining how it was presented by them (and how their understanding was received by me, it must be added). It helps perhaps to look back at the discussion of gender stereotypes and how such 'models' for male and female could be seen and usefully applied. We can see males as having, through whatever means, more characteristics accepted as 'masculine' than women have, but not an exclusive right to them nor a total absence of 'feminine' traits. In the same way, how women saw rape was not exclusively personal or impersonal, nor did the same women feel the same all through coping with victimisation. However, overall, some women clearly saw the reason for the rape as more personal than impersonal and vice versa.

Women also had a variety of ways of seeing what this meant. Yvonne, for example, saw the rape as a personal attack, but she believed it could have happened to anybody and she was not to blame. However, she did think that the rapist singled her out because she was a vulnerable target, and because she was forever being picked on by the authorities or those likely to do her harm. Fiona did not blame herself either but felt that other people did. She also felt that the rapist was punishing her in particular and so felt it was a personal attack. Sara thought that the rapists had picked out their chance rather than picked on her. She therefore felt the experience as impersonal. A personal attack, the women felt, was one where the rapist wanted to harm them in particular, for whatever reason.

Half the women in this study saw the rape as a personal attack and twelve showed some type of depression in the first few months following the assault. Eight had some type of sexually transmitted disease, pregnancy or injuries to cope with which tended to keep the attack more in the present than allowing it to become the past, and focused their feelings about the attack on themselves and the damage that had been done. From the women's accounts, a variety of factors were compared to see how they related to the personal/impersonal split (Fig. 4.1). Some did and some did not seem relevant to the women defining their experience in this way:

Number of Women

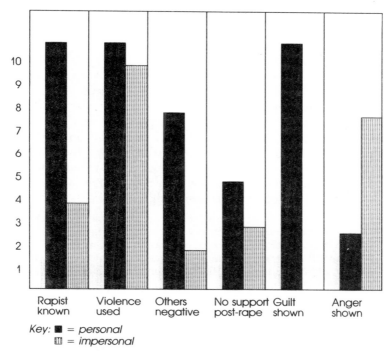

Figure 4.1 Factors considered for personal/impersonal view of attack

Knowing the rapist

This would seem to be the obvious factor which women would see as defining whether or not the rape was a personal attack, but not all of the women who were raped by men they knew took it to mean that the rape was aimed specifically at them. However, focusing on the prior contact with the rapist, and through this the pre-rape situation, indicated that it was not so much any relationship with the rapists which mattered, but a breaking of trust which in part at least made women feel they had been picked on for something they had done, or that the rapists believed they had done. There was also an element of feeling that others might be more on the side of the rapist(s) than supporting them:

Fiona cut all friends who knew both her and the rapist out of her life, because she felt they had betrayed her by letting them meet, and she believed that the mutual friends sided with the rapist. She felt that he had intended the evening to end with sex and when she clearly didn't follow his intention, he raped her as a punishment.

Women who did not know their rapists before the rape, or who had perhaps met them only at the 'pre-rape' situation, could be left with the question 'why pick on me?' and so start to focus responsibility for the assault on themselves. Even where they understood that the rapist could have picked on any other woman, the fact that he did not was still a worry. The idea of any man turning into a rapist was as big a betrayal of trust as a friend or relative suddenly turning. Some other women, who clearly knew their rapists, reasoned differently:

Bea, who was raped by her brother-in-law, never blamed anyone but him. She was well supported by her husband, and chose not to involve any of the rest of her family except to make sure she never had to be in the same gathering as him again. She was pregnant as a result of the rape but didn't allow it to affect her conviction that she had done nothing to provoke him, that she did nothing wrong and that it was not going to ruin her happy life.

The essential difference between a personal and impersonal attack appeared to focus on whether the woman saw that there was something inherently bad about the men who raped them, or whether they believed that something about them, or their own actions, could have made a man or men hurt them.

Extra violence during the rape

This was one element which appeared at first to influence whether the woman saw the rape as personal or impersonal, by leaving physical injuries as well as intensifying the experience of rape by violent physical abuse. However, whether extra vio- lence was part of the rape or not was the product of too complex a mesh of factors to provide a straightforward factor to assess.

Alice was immobilised with shock when a trusted man turned on her. Given that the rapist did not seem to want to use violence for its own ends, he did not need to use more than enough force to complete the sexual assault. **Yvonne** did fight, and was physically hurt because her rapist was willing to beat her into submission. **Olivia** could not and did not even struggle and she was physically hurt too, seemingly because her rapist wanted to hurt and humiliate her. **Norma** was brutalised by a rapist who did not need to use any violence, if all he had wanted was sex, but he too seemed to need to be brutal. **Barbara** and **Enid** were both unconscious so were immobilised by violence – **Barbara** was physically damaged; **Enid** was not. **Hilda** was immobilised by shock of a sudden attack by a total stranger, **Patience** was young and intimidated by an older man, and in neither situation was violence used. In **Una**'s case, she was in hospital and incapable even of voluntary movement. It was clear that her rapist was using the situation to commit rape without needing to resort to extra violence.

Where a gang was involved, extra violence usually accompanied the rape and seemed to indicate, as with some single or pair rapes, that physical abuse was part of the rapists' plan.

Gemma was badly abused and humiliated as part of the attack by a gang she didn't know. **Charlotte** was treated with contempt by the gang who raped her, not as if they intended to hurt her specifically, but as if they didn't care whether she was hurt or not. **Diana** made the conscious decision not to 'give them the satisfaction' of struggling. She remained very controlled and aloof and felt this had reduced her physical injuries.

The main difficulty in looking at violence was actually what was meant by the term. Rape itself is violent, some women saw one blow as more than necessary to define their assailant as violent, and others who sustained injuries did not describe the attack as particularly violent. Whatever assessment was made, whether based on the women's own definition or a grading of injuries or the description of the assault, there was little difference betwen those who saw their experience as personal or impersonal.

Others' reaction to the rape

This consideration really started to show what women saw as important to their understanding of what happened to them. During the immediate post-rape situation, the women were already beginning to define what had happened to them in terms of 'what will others think about this?' Where women decided not to involve someone close to them because they feared or didn't want to face the response, or where those informed reacted badly towards the women, then women were more likely to believe that they had been picked on for some reason personal to them:

Sandy didn't just think that the rapist had picked on her in particular, he had told her so. He was an ex-boyfriend and, although they had never had a sexual relationship, he resented it when she stopped seeing him. He threatened to 'get' her father if she ever told anyone what had happened. Given he had just 'got' her and hurt her, there was no reason for her to disbelieve him. She was six months pregnant before her mother finally made her tell her what had happened. She was still very fearful that the rapist would find out and carry out his threat, and she felt guilty for bringing such trouble on her family. When a doctor and counsellor she saw about an abortion both seemed to disbelieve her, she became more withdrawn than ever and started to deny it herself. Only with the support of her mother, and a very sympathetic medical team who finally performed a late abortion for her, could she acknowledge both her experience and the fear she had carried afterwards.

Jo had the police almost laugh at her, and her husband frightening her with his own anger at what had happened. What she didn't have was much support for her own feelings. She was angry and ashamed and distressed, but she could show little. Her family background was very rigid, and she found it difficult anyway to release her feelings. She found it necessary to hide what was happening to her, for fear that someone else would let her down. What came out in part was that she felt she had let herself down also, and, once again, the 'English middle-class-family' was in her own head telling her she must have done something to cause her own victimisation.

Where women began to feel that the rape had nothing to do with them personally, others tended to confirm this view, or would have confirmed the view if they had been asked:

Dulcie leaned heavily on her family and friends and found them able to take it. She was angry that the courts had not vindicated her experience: the rapist had pleaded guilty to 'attempted rape' but she did not feel relieved at not having to face the court – she had been raped and wanted that acknowledged. Luckily, she had others around who let her use that anger constructively to aim it outwards at the rapist and the system and not inwards at herself.

No support post-rape

This was another factor which seemed as if it should be relevant but wasn't. Again, the complex mesh of reasons behind why a woman would seek or not seek support immediately after the rape, and who she would turn to, made the simple factor 'no support' too simple. However, in focusing on it, the decision-making process women went through post-rape was brought out.

In thinking about who to tell and why, women often described a kind of internal dialogue, where each person relevant to them or the situation (like the police, for example) would be brought to mind and considered. 'What do I know of them? If I told them, what would they say or do? Would that be good or bad? If I don't tell them, then how would I feel? Will they find out anyway? Then what would happen?' Very quickly, the decision emerges based on 'to best help myself, what do I do now?' This is not to say that such rationalisation was always put into practice – some women had determined to tell no-one but couldn't hide it when faced with a concerned or cared-for person who looked at them and said 'Are you alright?' or 'What's happened?' One woman, explaining why she had told her mother, when she had firmly decided not to, said 'Not telling her was different from lying to her, when she said "what's happened", I couldn't say "nothing".' Where women were totally out of control post-rape, for example when injured and taken to hospital, the decision-making process could still be gone through, but they had little opportunity to see it work out.

Guilt or anger

These were the two factors which most clearly helped to show how the women defined their experience.

Where women felt that the rape was a personal assault, expressions of guilt were common; as if in trying to understand why someone would attack them in that way, the women had to find answers in themselves. Guilt was at times a way of trying to get the situation under control, for if a woman could believe she was in some way responsible, she could perhaps avoid it happening again. Once control was established, guilt and self-blame were no longer needed. However, guilt was sometimes an expression of how the woman saw herself, her right to control her own situation and her understanding of what others thought of her. Where a woman felt that she was more destructive than her assailant, guilt tended to compound the feeling of lack of control and undermined her.

Where women were able to express anger at their victimisation, their focus and their feelings were aimed outwards, setting blame firmly on the rapist and not themselves. Anger could be difficult to deal with: it was not uncommon for women to feel that their rage was tearing them apart because, without actually turning on the rapist, it had no legitimate target. Where women were able to use their anger to sustain them, to reassure them that the rapists had not 'won' or beaten them spiritually, then even undirected at the rapist, it could be constructive. In a sense, women used their anger at times to gain self control because, as long as they were angry, no-one could hurt them again. Women also expressed anger in different ways: defiantly, in controlled bursts, in outbursts, and assertively.

In looking at anger, guilt and depression, and the personal/ impersonal view of the experience of victimisation, one other emotional stand which was adopted became clear. Diana had said that she had appeared unconcerned during the rape so as not to give the rapists the satisfaction of seeing how frightened she was, and in doing that she won the mental battle. Bea remarked that the worst thing that she could do if her rapist ever mentioned the rape would be to say 'that? I never think about it', for in dismissing his assault she would be dismissing him, and for him to feel ineffective would be the worst punishment. In these ways, these women managed to work with their feelings and accept the experience as having happened but over with, a part of history. Whatever their overall response, in sorting out what the experience meant to them, women were coping with it and working through and out of victimisation – whatever kind of victimisation they eventually understood to have been imposed on them.

UNDERSTANDING THE RAPE EXPERIENCE AS A TYPE OF VICTIMISATION

A major reason for doing this study was to gain an insight into how women understand their own experiences of rape, in order to provide information about the kind of support most needed. What became clear was how important the responses of others, and society for that matter, was to women who had been raped and how much difference a clear supportive, positive response could make to a woman's self image and her view of her experience of rape. The factors involved in victimisation gradually formed a picture of how women saw themselves and their experiences, until what emerged from the accounts was the 'type' of victimisation they felt they had gone through.

The first factor which emerged as a indicator of different types of victimisation was whether women saw the assault as *personal* or *impersonal.* In reviewing the accounts of these thirty women, what also became clear was how guilt and anger were almost opposing factors; they were a key way that women showed how they felt.

Beginning with those women who saw their victimisation as personal, when asked to describe how they felt the commonest answer was *betrayed.* Whether by the rapists, the system, those around them or themselves, the women felt that one of the many things that had been abused during the whole process was their trust:

Barbara had no-one to turn to by the end of the first month after the rape. She lost her job, her lover, and got close to losing herself. Only one friend stayed by her, giving whatever support he could. And the RCC. The police were disinterested, she had injuries, VD and pregnancy to deal with. When she asked 'why me?' it really was asking why someone had tried to destroy her. It took some time, but eventually her self-respect healed, she became involved in a new career, and felt things were really improving when she became involved with a woman who made it clear she could understand what had happened and wanted to be supportive.

Charlotte was one of the women who had a lingering question – was she set up by boys she knew and trusted? She was in a confused and unsteady situation at the time she was raped. She had left home and was trying to cope on her own. After the rape, she turned to her mother, who did take care of her, but Charlotte resented it. After VD, pregnancy, an abortion and turning to drugs, she said the rape left her feeling like a 'monster'. She held the world in contempt for what it had done to her. Two years after the rape, there were slight improvements. She was under treatment for depression, holding steady then reducing her heroin use, learning to trust others and not abuse her parents for caring for her. For her, the victimisation really had gone on a long time.

Enid was shattered at having everything she believed in ruined. Unable to focus her bitterness outwards, she took it out on herself. She despised anyone who tried to help, because she believed that no one who she had any respect for would waste their time with her. Her feelings were partly that the rapist(s) must have chosen her because they recognised something awful in her, and partly that, whatever she was before, she had changed. When she found that she was pregnant, she described the pregnancy as 'the parasite they left behind'. Although she had loving support, she didn't feel she could accept it. Gradually, the patience of her family paid off and she started to come out of herself and challenge the despair. A year after the rape, she was cautious about her feelings. She still didn't see her life ever taking up the settled, normal, 'so safe' course it had been on before, but she was beginning to feel she had some part to play.

Jo felt betrayed by her background. She believed that the 'be quiet, don't make any fuss, nice girls don't' lifestyle she had been brought up with had silenced her when she needed to shout, had blinded her when she needed to see the warning signals, and had frozen her when she had needed to protect herself. At first, she wanted someone to take care of her, but when those around her failed to do so, she wanted only to sleep, to become so totally inert that nothing she did would prompt anyone to hurt her again. She was bitter that the rape had damaged her physically; bitter that she hadn't been believed; mistrusted the friends who had introduced her to the rapist; felt that her life had been left full of fear. She asked for something to stop her feeling. Although she wanted to talk and get her feelings out, she was as much afraid of that as of the rapist seeing her again. She had never been allowed to express her feelings, and couldn't just develop the skill because she needed to. She consciously decided to push the memory and experience away rather than deal with it, because she couldn't do anything else. She did, however, make drastic changes in her life, giving herself more independence, which gave her some confidence that she wouldn't remain quite as vulnerable as she felt.

Norma saw herself in no other way but as a partner to a man. She felt unsafe without a man around, spent all her social time with men and thought that only through a man could she achieve a social status. When the rape cut her off from men, and destroyed the basis of her security in her life and herself, she was distraught. When the police treated her unsympathetically, and the court found her rapist not guilty, and she found herself totally isolated, she had to begin to think again. Gradually, she started by looking for company in non-dating situations – adult education and dancing where she had reason other than looking for a man for being there. She had been estranged from her father, and believed that he too would reject her if he knew what had happened, but when she told him, he was upset and angry for her and very supportive. That new relationship she developed with him helped her self-confidence in sorting out a space for herself where she felt she was legitimate, where she didn't have to either ask a man's permission to exist or expect a man's violence for doing so.

Terri felt betrayed by the system. She hated the fact that she had been left alone to support a child when her ex-husband went off; she hated and feared the estate she lived in, and had tried hard to be moved to somewhere she would feel more secure. She was upset when the police were so dismissive, and knew that they were reacting to their beliefs about the people on that estate and not to her. She had tried to talk to her rapist, but could not get him to see her as a human being with feelings. With the stresses of sole responsibility of a child, struggling to manage on benefit and living in fear in her own home, the rape was just one more experience which proved she was disregarded. Only her mother, who stayed angry and supportive right through her daughter's distress, helped to keep her together. When the police suddenly became more interested, because they picked the rapist up on another charge, Terri had come through enough to get angry. She saw she had a right to be believed the first time, not to have to wait for someone to find out she had mattered and was telling the truth.

Una felt betrayed by the situation she was in. Hospitalised because of exhaustion while travelling, the helplessness of her situation when she was raped accentuated the fact that she had been somewhere she should have felt safe and was hurt instead. As a child, she had family to reassure her that she had not caused her father's death, and who allowed her the space to work through her grief. She could lose control. She was raped while travelling alone, in a totally strange country, and didn't have space to explore her feelings. She wanted to go home, to fall into the middle of that family and let her bitterness out. She knew that she was unlikely to ever be able to face travelling again and that saddened her. She was angry enough to say 'I won't give that bastard the satisfaction of letting his rape hurt me', but also vulnerable enough to know it had done. Once back with her family, she was able to let go. Until then though, she really felt the rapist had destroyed her trust in her own ability to cope with strangeness.

Through these expressions of betrayal, the women focused on several factors connected with the experience of victimisation through rape. The first was the breaking of trust, not just in those who committed rape but in the normal, everyday situations and relationships from which rape had developed. Where women had seen their role as dependants, or had looked to men for protection and identity, then the rape was a real attack on their femaleness. Where women were living independent of men, or trying to, or where they felt rejected by men, then they felt the rape as a punishment, a pushing them back into line.

Connected to this view of rape as either an attack on the vulnerability of femininity, or as a sanction against those not sticking to the rules, was the idea these women had that the rape had changed them in some way. Some of the women, like Una, recognised this and challenged it, others could not. If they couldn't quite believe that they had been essentially bad before, then they did see that the rape had spoilt them in very fundamental ways. If being a 'good' woman had been a major source of security, then it was no longer there and some other security needed to be found. If being different was the target for such abuse, then at times the difference itself became the problem.

Two of the women found it difficult to focus their understanding of the rape on anyone but themselves. For different reasons, they did not feel betrayal by anyone, but only believed that they were entirely *guilty*:

Sandy had picked up enough messages about what a nice girl does or doesn't do to know that calling around to see an ex-boyfriend would be seen as provocative. That she was tricked made little difference, she thought she should have known better (no, he'd never been known to do anything like that to her before). His parting words terrified her, he just overpowered her, which she never imagined could or would happen, and when he threatened her father, who was ill, she had no reason to doubt that he would be able to carry out his threat. The message she received was that if she talked to anyone, it would be her fault if her father got hurt. The disbelief of a doctor and counsellor added to the fear – if her ex-boyfriend hadn't raped her, then she had hurt herself, or made him hurt her. She made the comment to her mother that only the fact that she was pregnant convinced her that she hadn't imagined the whole thing. The fact that she was believed by her family, that she did get help and support from others, and her father survived, was the final key in allowing her to shed her guilt, get angry and put the whole thing behind her.

Iris had been taught early on to feel guilty, so was inclined to take the blame for the rape on herself. This process was helped by the negative response from the police and hospital, who seemed more concerned with the disruption to routine than with her, and a brutal assault which she thought no-one would commit against another human being (therefore, goes the logic of guilt, 'I am not a human being'). To cope, she lived behind a facade – desperate to be helpful and to please, while convinced people would find out that she was bad. The guilt, not just from the rape but from her background, undermined her in many ways, until she had the space and time to deal with the rape and its meaning for her. When she also accepted support and how much others really valued her, and saw in her work and experiences value in her own right, then the guilt began to recede as a controlling force in her life. It was a long and rocky process, but she made it.

The problem with guilt is that it is unrealistic. Although there is a sense of safety that goes with assuming that one is responsible for everything that happens, it is a false sense of security and so unstable., The problem is that lack of trust in others is translated into lack of trust in oneself. Sandy hoped that by taking it all on herself she could protect her father. Iris couldn't protect anyone, including herself. Both were in dependent relationships with their families, both were young and so measuring their worth very much by what was reflected back to them by others. They both needed support and validation before they could deflect the guilt and the victimisation.

For a few of the women it seemed that the victimisation process went beyond how they responded but became instead a status which, temporarily, took over their lives. Where women saw the rape as a personal attack, they often felt, at some point, changed by the experience. For some this change included a feeling of security that 'being a victim' gave to them. Although seeming to be not in control of their lives, these women controlled passively by losing themselves in victimisation.

What marked this response was the response to incidents and situations after the rape, and response to others. Any problem, conflict or difficulty, however small, could become a crisis, and help and attention would be elicited on that basis. In dealing with others, there would be a very upfront acknowledgement of problems and painful memories, but an effective block on anyone trying to offer support or change. When talking to women about their lives before the rape, it was apparent that there was a kind of continuity. Though the response to the rape itself was highly disruptive, in fact women described their lives as a continuous series of crises. There was no suggestion that any of the problems or crises were self-induced, only that once something upsetting had happened, the safest path seemed to be to lose themselves in it. This made other people take over and provided a barrier against further pain. The problem with this *total victimisation* response, for the women going through it, was that they took control of their lives by being out of control, acting only through the ways in which they could make others respond to them. It was a dangerous state, utterly dependent, and made sure that the cycle of crises, victimisation and reaction repeated itself:

Fiona saw nothing reassuring in her comfortable surburban lifestyle. In talking about her life, she described a series of incidents and experiences which were damaging and distressing to her, which she saw as connected to how she experienced the rape. She had suffered depression for years, and felt trapped rather than nurtured by her family and situation. The first few months after the rape were marked by a series of crises which continually brought the rape back to the forefront of her thoughts. Although the incidents themselves would not be self-created, her response to them often made matters worse (not taking care of herself when she was ill, or getting into arguments with people who were clearly unsympathetic or unreasonable). At the same time, she rejected any response from others which offered a possibility of change. Her fear was not unfounded – her experience was that many straightforward situations turned into nightmares. Her long-term depression was an expression of her feeling that she could trust no-one, including herself, and that there was no way out. A year after the rape, there were signs that this was changing. She left her husband and family, and consciously started again. It was a fragile confidence she had in herself, but with support from new friends around her, it seems to be holding.

Yvonne took on victimisation in a slightly different way. She had lived with disturbance from early childhood. She was sexually abused by her father and brother, her sister committed suicide in a psychiatric unit when both were in their early teens, and Yvonne for most of her adolescence and adulthood had been using drugs. At 25, she was used to being one step ahead of both the health and police authorities. She was used to having to depend on others, and to use that dependence to her own ends. But the rape shook her badly. Whatever else she faced, and whatever type of people she mixed with, never had she faced such brutality as she did in the rape, and never been betrayed in quite such a total way. The judge in the trial pointed out in his summing up that, whereas the defence had tried to use her background and history as a reason for disbelieving her, it only showed that she was vulnerable and had a right to protection. Yvonne in some ways saw the investigation and court case as a test for herself. Her response to victimisation or trouble had always been to block it or disappear and start again. The six months between the rape and the court case were marked with drug excesses, self-violence, spells in a psychiatric unit, and escapes from the same. The worst attempt at self-harm came after the court case was over, and the rapist found guilty. The effect of seeing her experience taken out of her hands and used by the authorities she had fought for years was, in the end, too much for her. She also saw the 'end' to her experience as a loss – 'you won't want to see me any more, will you, I mean, I'm not a rape victim any more.' She became instead another kind of victim and added more scars to her body. But, somewhere in the confusion, she also saw that she had, for once, seen something through to the end, and survived. She did disappear, but resurfaced about a year later, seeming to have a good chance at really changing. A spell in a small therapeutic community, as a volunteer, and the friendship of a priest who she saw as being interested in her as a person not as a soul, at least had given her a few months' rest and the chance for some of the physical and emotional scars to heal.

Rose was pushed into being taken over by the victim role. Labelled as different by her family, and in many ways used by them as the repository of conflict and problems, ignored most of the time, and experiencing normal routine as isolation, Rose learned that to get attention she had to over-react, to force a crisis. The rape was a real crisis which left her feeling possessed and hunted, and literally took control of her life away from her. She had to rely on others to cope for her when she went hysterical. They didn't. Instead, her family and friends grew tired of her needs and withdrew support. She had no reserves of self-respect to call on when she was left to cope alone, and so tried to kill herself within a few weeks of the rape. This was again responded to as a minor irritation by those around her. Rose became convinced that she could and had provoked evil, and was trapped in a spiral of pain and the need to have that pain recognised. Her self-image was bad or non-existent, her only power the power to hurt herself. At times, only the RCC were giving her any other messages. Eventually, she stood back and reassessed what was happening and began to see how much of her negative self-image was imposed on her by others, and slowly looked for other models, and a new direction which would provide a firmer base on which to build her own life; one she could believe in for herself.

Gemma was trapped by her belief that she could not change her situation, and perhaps she was right. She was brutally raped by a gang of young men but had no outlet other than the RCC for working through it or protecting herself. She could not leave work, because she had no other means of support, which meant having to face the situation of the rape daily. She couldn't tell her husband because he was a violent man and she didn't trust him with her vulnerable feelings – she believed he would hurt her more. She therefore couldn't tell the authorities and protect herself or seek help in any way. She was stuck. She could never work through her feelings, using counselling only to cope when she panicked or her feelings became too much. She stopped calling either when the crises stopped or when the focus of her fear changed. I doubt it was because she truly stopped feeling victimised.

Olivia dropped out of sight when faced with a choice between continued vulnerability and trying to do something about her situation. She was involved with drugs, lived precariously in squats, and had had a series of unsatisfactory relationships. She had been abused as a child, left handicapped by an accident, and, as with Yvonne, grown into her adult life manipulating and avoiding welfare and police authorities. She was raped by a man who felt slighted because she had the nerve to say she didn't want to sleep with him, and Olivia could see that in her life, she could rarely with safety make such decisions for herself. She couldn't face the court case, or seeing through the consequences of her victimisation. She hadn't chosen to inform the police but was too hurt to stop it happening. Her injuries and the involvement of others meant that she remained out of control of her situation long after the rape had actually ended. She was used to having to act through others, or leaving it to others to define what she was doing and with who. Her only way of regaining any semblance of control was to disappear, which she did, resurfacing some months later – in another area, hassled by new authorities, in a new but essentially familiar situation of insecure housing, finances and people.

When women described the rape as an 'impersonal' attack, there was a feeling of being detached, as if the women were able to distance themselves in some ways from the victimisation process. The essential point they made was that the rape had nothing to do with them as individuals. They did not cause it or prompt it, unless by existing, and all responsibility and blame stayed firmly with the rapists. At the most, women saw that they were *accident* victims; as with an accident, they saw it could have been anyone (or at least any woman) and they could recover:

Pru acknowledged that it was a bad accident, but refused to let it get any further into her life than that. She left the country it had happened in, refusing to extend the effect by participating in a criminal case. She did successfully leave the rape behind to a great extent, but realised there were some lasting effects. Her mistrust of men, stemming in part from the man who betrayed her trust by taking her to the rapists, settled her into her sexual life as a block which prevented her trusting men with her sexual feelings. She could recognise this effect without assuming any permanent or damaging change within herself.

Sara was able to use her friends' support to see that she was still the young woman they loved and the rape was no more than a bad experience. She was hurt by the rape, and showed her pain through reactions such as fear of crowds and panic attacks. She was able to adjust her life to feel secure again without making protection against further assault a restriction or obsession. She also had a sense of herself as worth the concern and love, an indication of the support she drew on from her family.

Katy was thrown back into the fear of the rape attack when she heard noises as if someone was breaking into her flat, as the rapist had done, though then she had not heard him. She had good support from her mother and was able to get angry about her situation. She knew that she was vulnerable (she was disabled and living alone) but saw that the rapist had taken advantage of her vulnerability because he chose to, that victimisation was not inevitable. She did have a bad time again when the noises brought the whole thing back, but she was able, once more, to recover.

Vi, in the main, saw her situation as being the unfortunate woman 'some nut' picked on. She was angry at the rapist, angry at the police, and furious when he was acquitted. She never doubted she knew what had happened to her, and her husband remained supportive throughout.

Anni could never understand why a man she saw as a friend turned on her, but had to accept that he had. She believed it showed some dreadful side of his character, and proceeded with her life according to that belief. She retaliated, ensuring that he did not get away with it through her silence, and seeing her action in declaring what he had done and getting his crime known among their friends as both therapeutic for herself and preventive. She saw that he had abused her trust, but reasoned that by declaring him a rapist, no other woman would ever trust him again.

Bea made a comment which summed up her attitude towards her own victimisation, and showed why she could feel detached from the whole experience of rape:

> My husband said that his brother was always selfish and stupid. I don't know why he did it, but I think the worst thing I could do now, if he ever tried to mention it, because he's arrogant and might, would be to say 'Good grief, I'd forgotten all about it'.

Effy needed her friends and especially her mother to understand the shock and disbelief she felt at being raped by a man she knew. She saw his actions as odd and not her own, unless being nice was odd, which she did tend to feel on her bad days. Her trust in others, especially men, was badly shaken, but support and, in a way, her own disbelief helped to provide the distance which allowed her to see it as something which was over with and which she would get over.

There was no difference in severity, and no significant differences between the women themselves when it came to who felt the rape as personal and who didn't. Those who saw the rape as an accident were able to use some aspect of their situation or the assault to stand back from the victimisation. They asked 'why me?', but the most important question was: 'how do I get through this?' The big difference seemed to revolve around the way that these women felt and expressed their anger. Only by degree, and with little actually between them, some women managed to use that anger to dismiss victimisation altogether. Where some were overwhelmed by the status and situation of being a victim, others said 'me, I'm *not a victim* – at all':

Diana began her stand against being a victim when she struggled to remain cool and aloof in the face of the rapists' assaults and jeers. She let go with her feelings when with her friends, but knew that she would remain in control, that she was not vulnerable to them. She had problems with her father, who wanted to take over and 'deal' with it himself, and with her mother whose response was to go to pieces. Diana knew, without realising, that her strength lay in refusing to feel victimised. Her confidence was shaken when she failed her exams, but she realised when she talked it through that she could not go through an experience like that without being affected in some way. She went away before the end of the trial, not caring what the law did to the rapists. She saw the court case as a need to defend herself again and prepared for that as a fight against victimisation too. The satisfaction for her came with knowing that they – rapists, police, courts, her father – had not broken her will.
Hilda saw the rape not as a personal assault but as part of the web of male/female relations. She said that she was glad that she was a part of the women's movement because she found feminist understanding both comforting and compatible to her own situation. She thought about who to tell and why, and got the support she needed from those she did confide in. The police were good to her, and she was able to both give and get support with another woman attacked by the same man. She wouldn't walk along the same path again, but saw that as a small matter. She said also, about a year after the rape, that she began to be aware of the potential for rape in everyday situations with men and was consciously trying to get her relationships on a more secure and determined footing. In a sense, in refusing to be a victim to a rapist, she began to ensure that she would not be any kind of victim again.

Lianne had shown her own awareness of the potential danger facing young women when she had warned a friend to come and see how she was if she didn't return in a few minutes. She was angry at the boy who betrayed her, at the gang who assaulted her and the police who then acted as if it was her fault. She was in conflict with the authorities anyway, having run away from care, but did have adults around her who were caring and supportive, and allowed her to express her feelings. A few months after the rape, she made a quite conscious decision never to be vulnerable again. She recognised that violence was a part of her community, that women were treated like dirt and decided that the rape was the last time anyone would abuse her. She began to focus on her education, seeing in that a way to use her own intelligence and to protect her from being classed as useless.

Wanda fought the whole way through the rape and had to continue to fight afterwards. She was angry from the start, at the boys who attacked her, and though she cried and went into uncontrollable shaking, inside she was determined that they wouldn't break her. Her foster parents and her own father helped her to see that she had a right to be angry and gave her space to feel. The police were hostile and she threw their hostility back in their faces. Her mother resented the trouble but Wanda coped with that as part of their difficult relationship. When she cornered one of the boys who had assaulted her, and scared the life out of him, she really turned the tables – saying 'I'm not your victim, not at all'.

Whereas Diana and Hilda worked on their own anger and assertiveness in a very controlled way, Wanda and Lianne, younger and already at odds with society, snapped into anger and so set their course through victimisation. Hilda had a theoretical understanding of women's situation to work with, the two younger women used their personal experience of girls at risk. All were in a way rejecting the feminine stereotype or model for action when deciding that, whatever they suffered, rape was surmountable.

For two women, their understanding of the rape, and how they felt it, was less clearly understood in the terms I have used so far:

Alice felt the rape had been aimed at her personally, it disrupted every close relationship she had, and created turmoil where she believed she had things sorted out. The family of her lover's father, who was the man who raped her, split down the middle, some believing him and some her. The fact that her lover never wavered helped her self-esteem tremendously, but the rape became a crisis for both of them in the end. A pre-planned but well-timed move away to a new job, so away from their families, gave them both a fresh start and signalled the end to having to cope with the rape as part of her life, because it could become a part of the past.

Dulcie had a strong understanding of her victimisation as impersonal, and she had support which also helped her to keep in mind that the rapist was responsible for his own actions, not her. She in many ways saw herself as a 'non-victim', as a woman used by a man but not broken – until the rape was denied as a crime. Her experience was then taken out of her hands, defined as sexual assault not rape and when the rapist pleaded guilty she was not even required to attend the court case which had hung over her. Dulcie was furious, feeling that the police had denied her own experience, 'it was rape, not almost rape,' was her constant cry. Although the police had acted in the hope of saving her a court case, the mislabelling of her experience and feelings left Dulcie feeling betrayed – first by the rapist who used her trust to do her harm, but mostly by the system which allowed him to get away with a lesser charge, and left her unvindicated.

There were two other women, Cathy and Patience, whose situations meant that their responses to victimisation were less clearly understood:

Cathy was schizophrenic. Although she clearly had been raped, what was less certain was when. At times it seemed as if it had happened shortly before she made contact, and the assault had produced a crisis, but later in counselling it seemed possible that the rape which she spoke of had occurred in the past, and another incident had brought it back to her. Cathy struggled with her feelings for a few weeks, then returned to a psychiatric unit she had been in before. She maintained contact while in hospital and when she came out, over her crisis and stable once more, Cathy was vulnerable because she had no measure for trusting people. Eventually, she became involved with another ex-patient of the unit and they seemed to be able to give each other support and protection.

Patience was never allowed to respond when the rape occurred and found it difficult in her adult situation to reconnect with her feelings as a girl. She showed clearly the difficulties faced by women who kept their rape experience secret for years. Patience was quite isolated, feeling that there was no space in life for herself and also believing that she did not need such space. She was dealing with shut in but insistent feelings from the rape, problems within her marriage, and social isolation. She didn't resolve much in counselling, except that she had the space to at least look at the problems and talk about the experience. That in itself took away some of the confusion and gave her a clear view in tackling the rest.

Although there were similarities in how women understood their experiences of sexual violence, the thirty accounts used here also show that for each woman rape was a unique experience. Their difference and the wide range of responses the

women used to express their feelings, was the clearest reason
why the one term 'victim' can only reduce an individual's experience and creates a false picture of one single social status.

An interesting issue which emerged, looking through all
contact with the thirty women, was that they expressed their
experiences differently at different times in the whole process.
Details would be changed, perhaps whether a weapon was used
or what kind of violence inflicted. It was apparent that women
actually remembered different things at different times, or
experienced the memory as different. For example, when a
woman is focusing on her sexual feelings, she may not relate the
added violence she suffered. At another time, she may be
focusing on her fear of pain and so the violence comes to the fore.
This made it even more important to move away from comparing facts and descriptions and move towards seeing the rape
experience as a total process of victimisation – because it was
closer to how the women saw rape, not how anyone outside the
experience defines it.

The range of situations the women described being in before
the rape occurred, and from which the rape developed at times,
was one indication of the way that rape can be seen as a part of
normal social interaction. For the women, such normality at
times was one reason why their response to rape included a
significant mistrust of men, people, friends or normality at all.

The immediate post-rape situation can be marked for women
by a feeling of remaining out of control of their situation or can
be the point where women can take stock and make decisions
about their future. It is from this point, sometimes within hours
of the rape, that others around the woman can play a crucial
role. They can influence a woman into hiding her response, into
letting her feelings out, into taking charge of her own responses,
or into feeling overwhelmed by either well-meaning but in-
trusive support, or denial and rejection. Victimisation high-
lights the ongoing process of understanding ourselves through
reflection.

In coping with rape, women are actually coping with a social
definition and reaction to rape and to victims. Being a victim,
like being the 'ideal woman', is understood to be a passive,
reactive role. To become a victim, someone or something else
has to do something to you. Victimisation, how being a victim is
experienced, is anything but passive, just as living itself is

always an activity. Once through the initial act, these women were then in an active role where the point for them was to understand what had happened, deal with the consequences, perhaps protect themselves, and try to resume control of their lives.

There is an end to victimisation, or at least we all believe there is. There comes a point where the experience of rape is history and distant, where women can feel it is behind them, not with them any longer. For some of the women here, the rape may be replaced by another act or situation which recreated victimisation for them, for others, guilt and depression extended the time it took them to feel that the rape was becoming a part of the past. For some, a touch of anger or perhaps the support of others, allowed them to take a side step away from feeling victimised, by allowing them to say from the start: 'this rape was not my fault'. It certainly seemed that the process of victimisation began to end once that conclusion was reached.

5 THE MANY FACES OF RAPE/THE MANY WAYS OF FACING RAPE

Rape is an invention. Rape can be unimaginable.

(Susan Griffin, 1979, p. 47)

Focusing on how women deal with rape in their own lives doesn't explain rape, or even provide answers to the question of how to stop rape happening, but it is a step in the right direction. From the time when the Women's Liberation Movement first provided the space for women to talk about their experience, and when those women responded with mutual support, rape could be seen in a different light. Perhaps now we can see the effects of rape more clearly and see those who have suffered rape as more than voiceless passive victims. Some of us have even seen that the idea of the willing victim is nothing more than an excuse for male violence, used by society to deny women's pain, because to recognise the extent of rape and its effects would be to admit the dark side of male superiority. In the beginning of the feminist campaign against rape, women talked to exorcise their own experiences, but also often to help other women to see they were not alone. If we have not stopped rape, we have redefined it, we have faced it, and we have set up the structures to deal with it for ourselves.

What the focus on women's experience of rape provides us with are questions. To begin with, there are questions about what rape is, or means, or does. The answers begin to emerge more clearly when rape is seen not as a single act but as a process of victimisation. How a woman responds is her way of saying what she feels has happened to her, and what she feels she can do about it.

UNDERSTANDING RAPE VICTIMISATION THROUGH RESPONSE

Response can be viewed in three ways, depending on whether those doing the responding are seen in an active or passive light. Most simply, response is the total collection of reactions to rape as an act, produced by the act and not by the woman herself. This is the passive 'victim' we all understand and can pity or despise, depending on how we feel about weakness. If that seems harsh it is because it is a reflection of society's judgement. To be overpowered, to lose control, is seen as weakness, and we either feel that we should be protective of the weak and look after them, or we feel they shouldn't be that way and ought to help themselves. It is not surprising that women who have been raped may feel guilty – not because of anything they know they have done, but because they too can feel the social message that perhaps they brought it on themselves through weakness.

Widening this idea of response as a sum of reactions, so we can include response as an expression of the needs and feelings of the victimised woman. Although this still leaves the impression of a woman not in control of her actions, there is more of a sense of involvement, in that the reaction is to her feeling, and not entirely to the act.

The accounts used here show clearly that response also goes beyond reactions to the act of rape, and includes expressions of understanding, and ways of dealing with the effects of victimisation or at least making the situation possible to cope with. In this way, response can be seen as an activity which defines the process of victimisation that an individual woman goes through.

In the aftermath of an experience such as rape, there are unconscious or uncontrolled reactions, and there are situations which remain out of a woman's control. What is important is to be able to place these reactions and situations within the context of an active woman's understanding of what has happened to her and what she needs. For example, some women find that focusing on increased security and changing parts of their lives makes them feel stronger – they can see the changes as positive and feel that they are no longer being victimised. Here, the women are in control of their own situation. There is another side. Dean Kilpatrick (1981), in a paper on 'avoidance' in response to rape, noted that where women had changed their lives in order to avoid unpleasant reminders of the rape, then security measures and other actions could become more obsessive – out of the woman's control. In understanding victimisation then, the first task is to see how far an individual woman is defining her own response, and how far others or the situation are defining it for her.

To see response as an activity is to challenge the view of women as passive objects and the view of 'victim' as a passive status. It may be valid to recognise in theory that passivity is an important part of the defining of femininity and victimisation, but the real question is whether passivity is experienced as such. Being out of control or overpowered, which is the experience, is different from being inert – which is what passivity sounds like.

The accounts of the women in this study made some very clear and important statements about rape. Reviewing their experiences, it immediately becomes clear why the feminist response to rape was to redefine it from a sexual to a violent act. Whatever the view of the rapists, however sexual their intentions, the situation which rape developed from was clearly non-sexual for most of the women in this study. Their knowledge of the rapists was often of men in seemingly 'safe' and non-sexual roles. Even where there was the possibility of sexual contact, even in fact where a woman may have chosen sexual activity with a man, the women concerned had assumed that their choice would be considered. What was clear to all afterwards was that it didn't matter what was going on inside their heads or feelings – the rapists didn't care. What also became clear in looking back before the rape was that the rapists had at times taken great care to disguise their intentions, to manipulate trust and vulnerability to ensure that women had the least chance possible of seeing and understanding the real situation, and of getting out.

When it came to the assault itself, what these women described was an act of violence which used sex as a weapon even where sex was also the ultimate goal of the rapists. Domination, power and sex weaved a complex pattern through the women's understanding of what had happened to them, and what their assailants seemed to think they were doing.

In describing what was happening during the assault itself, disbelief, even as the rape took place, was common. From perfectly normal situations, rape itself was utterly unbelievable. Some women talked of feeling out of place or distant from what was happening, a reaction described by women in other studies too. For some women, the detachment was worked at, a determined effort to prevent the rapists taking control completely, for others, it was an automatic response, an attempt by the mind to protect itself from overwhelming pain. The women noted smells or sounds which stuck in their memories afterwards and at times became a focus for reaction. One common comment from the police used to be that women should not bathe before they had been to a police station as valuable evidence was lost. So many women talked of how bad the rapists smelled that it became more understandable to me that women's first reaction would be to try to wash the smell off themselves and hang the evidence.

When talking about what the rapists did or said, the women expressed the confusion which seemed at times deliberately induced. When words such as 'don't worry, you'll be all right' followed a beating and clearly preceded further assault, it was not surprising that women expressed a mixture of fear, anger and hope. When ending the assault, rapists often would ask to see women again, or express regret that he hadn't really enjoyed it, or asked if the woman had. Is it a ritual? Is it so difficult for men too to accept that what they have done is rape? Can some honestly think that forcing, threatening or beating women to have sex is normal, or OK? Or is it, as many women suspected, that the odd phrases which didn't fit the action were intended to confuse and disarm? Would a woman who had accepted a date with a man who rapes her feel less sure of her ground if she thinks about reporting her experience and calling it a crime?

Although the women here would say 'he/they must have been insane', it was a part of the unbelief rather than a real feeling that it was mental disturbance which made the rapists behave as they did (except in one situation, for Hilda, where her assailant was a repeat offender and was diagnosed as disturbed).

It was pointed out earlier that the process of victimisation may start with an assault but develops through a longer period of time where a woman begins to fit the rape experience into her life and to cope with it. Looked at over time, a pattern of response for the women here was similar to the patterns noted by Sutherland and Scherl (1970) and Burgess and Holmstrom (1957), i.e. that after a period of time where the rape was the central focus of a woman's concern, there was then a period where getting on with life became more important. At this point, which may be within a few weeks of the rape itself, women did not want to talk about their experience and often said they were trying to forget it. Often this stage was ended by an incident or fright which made the woman re-focus on the rape. This stage, where the rape is in the present but the woman wants it to become part of her history, seemed to be the most appropriate point to talk and where counselling is most useful – not in crisis, but as a conscious decision to 'deal with' the rape as an experience. Hidden response could delay this response, and clearly many women either have no opportunity to deal with the rape when it is appropriate for them, or deal with the experience in other ways.

Understanding victimisation through response is understanding an activity and a process. Victimisation becomes the overall effect on someone of an act which is forced on them against their will and which removes self-control. The process of victimisation involves reasserting that control and making the experience a part of history.

Rape is a life-threatening experience tied in with our understanding of femininity, male–female relations and sexuality. Women finding their voices to express the pain of rape has changed our understanding of it. Equally, what we learned about rape has influenced the view we have of women's lives, and explained a lot about the nature of oppression. Understanding rape as victimisation made us aware of the personal distress of rape, but equally, made us view rape as a social problem.

When explaining how rape occurs in this society of ours which cares so much for women, feminism looked to the way that women are treated in other situations. They saw that using women's bodies to sell goods, treating women as little more than attractive packaging, social approval of the equation women = sex, all provided a background of treating women as objects which made rape possible. Something that can be bought and used can be taken and abused. The connection between using women's bodies as a commodity and rape was made in a more direct way by some of the women also. In talking about their feelings over time, women often mentioned that they became angry or upset at sexist advertising. There was one advert around for a little while, which showed a cartoon woman in underclothes with the slogan 'juicy, fruity, fresh and cheap'. What it was advertising is irrelevant. It was mentioned several times by women who had been raped, who took it as a personal insult – 'it felt like that was what they were saying about me', was the common feeling.

In feminist understanding, the idea of feminism and mascu-line stereotypes figure strongly. The overall idea of passive female and active male has been used to explain inequalities of opportunity and status, as well as explaining how the victim–offender roles can be developed. The victim is seen as being in a totally passive role, acted upon entirely, while the offender is active and in control. Feminism has argued that the idea of the passive female is a myth, that women survive the stereotype by acting in non-direct ways because direct ways are denied them. The experience of these women indicated a similar situation, and a connection between the feminine stereotype and the poten-tial for victimisation. Women could not be totally passive at any point in the victimising process (unless they were actually unconscious during the assault), but found their possible courses of action blocked in many ways. Think of the way that housework is often seen as 'doing' nothing, then think of Terri in this study who tried to talk her rapist out of continuing with his assault, and was ignored, or of Yvonne who was asked, while still covered in bruises, why she couldn't stop the rape.

If we view a stereotype as a model which we can compare ourselves with, then it is possible to see how close any one of us ever fits the model created for us. No-one, really, is utterly feminine or masculine – not if they are real, or, in the case of femininity, alive. 'Passive action' is the specification of how to keep femininity running smoothly – a do-it-yourself handbook on how to be the 'perfect female'. The basic guidelines are: look to others, act through others, wait for others, be quiet, do not think for yourself. Being a victim has similar rules: look out for others, others act upon you, wait to be told what to do and feel, be quiet and grateful, do not think for yourself. The women here showed that in real life we cannot be 'perfect victims' any more than 'perfect females', and the various ways they actively responded to victimisation were reflected in the types of experience they described.

The types of victimisation described by the women were descriptions of images, and ways of rationalising rape. There were a number of statements within the types:

> I refuse to see this as a personal attack except in the way that I was hurt by it. The rapist is at fault and so is the society which sees in my body or my life something to attack.

This is the heart of feeling *not a victim*.

> The rape has nothing to do with me personally, though it hurt me. I was unlucky and need help/treatment to recover. Then I should forget the whole thing.

It was an *accident*.

> Please don't come too close or I will infect you with the disease that is me. The rapist(s) knew that I was bad and that's why he/they did it. I have no right to exist as I am. I'm sorry.

I felt at times with some women that only an instinctive wish to live made them contact the Rape Crisis Centre, and the biggest hurdle was to get them to accept that they were worth someone else's time. Their statement is painful and guilt-ridden.

> After this I will never trust a soul again. No-one comes near me, you're all as bad as each other.

There is a point, perhaps, where we are all *betrayed* through rape; only some women state it quite this clearly.

> The only way the world sees me is by it hurting me. It hurts me because I'm unprotected. The only way I can stop it hurting me is if others protect me. The only way others will protect me is if I'm hurt.

For women *stuck as 'victims'*, the statement shows the double bind of vulnerability.

What was important for all women, whatever the statement in their response to victimisation, was for them to see that they exist other than as victims, and that their existence, actions and needs are valid. Counselling can help, if it is there to help a woman face, interpret and take control of herself and her situation.

COUNSELLING AS A RESPONSE TO RAPE

Whatever kind of victimisation they felt they had suffered, the women in this study had all asked for some kind of counselling support, sometimes years after the rape. What support was offered was very much directed by the women themselves, given that the approach of the Rape Crisis Centre was to give back the control over her life that a woman lost during rape. In practice this meant leaving it to the woman herself to define the help and support she wanted, and then to fit that as closely as we could. This viewpoint and basic strategy of counselling was the direct result of the feminist analysis of rape and the anti-rape movements. What this meant for the research was that counselling could be looked at as different types of support, because counselling was a direct response to the women themselves.

I doubt very much whether most of the women calling the Rape Crisis Centre cared very much whether the counsellors were feminist or not. What they were looking for were other women who would understand, and the Women's Movement supplied that understanding where the rest of society didn't. It was hard not to know that the Centre was at least 'different', certainly in the first few months of its existence. One national newspaper ran an article, after a reporter tricked her way into the Centre, calling the Rape Crisis Centre 'anti-man, anti-establishment and anti-police' (anti-newspapers we certainly became). One woman who called on the day this appeared said she felt real hope as she read this piece, because maybe we were anti-rapist too and that's what she needed. Only two of the women in this study would have defined themselves as feminist at the time they contacted the centre. All of them sought a place and people where their specific experience of rape would be understood and focused on.

Of the thirty women in this study, I was the main counsellor for thirteen, had some involvement with a further eleven and no direct contact with six. The small number of counsellors involved at the time, and the need for collective understanding of all the contacts with the RCC, did mean that knowledge of all these women, and others, was shared.

For two of the women, contact was primarily information-giving and referral on elsewhere, so a counselling relationship was minimal. For some of the others, where first contact was more than a year after the rape, a specific incident had sparked off feelings which had brought the rape back into the present in some way. For these women, counselling had little to do with how they had initially dealt with the rape, but served to help get their feelings and perceptions at the time of contact into perspective for them. The longer the time gap between the rape and contact with the RCC, the less likely that counselling would have an input into coping, except where responses had remained hidden until the contact, in which case coping itself could be delayed.

The counsellors' comments on what they felt about the relationship which was built up showed a wide variety of interactions. These comments included 'friendly', 'conspiritorial', 'a relationship of equals', 'mainly advisory', 'good as long as the counsellor was performing', and 'helping'. Eight different components of counselling were noted, either as major or overall relationships, or in combinations reflecting different demands at different times. Table 5.1 shows how many times each component came up in this study.

Table 5.1 Frequency of counselling components

Component	No. of occurrences
In-depth or involved support	9
Crisis support	8
Someone to talk to/back-up support	14
Advice	9
Counselling another involved	2
Alongside other therapy	2
Practical help	4
Dealing with rejecting support	3

In-depth or *involved support* meant that women saw the counselling from the RCC as a primary help in coping, at least some of the time. Here, women would use the counselling process to explore their feelings, their past and the experience. At times, the women would also use the RCC or the counsellor as they would a friend or other relationship, feeling free to lean at times. For example, going through the legal process could mean that the counsellor was useful as someone to hold on to in court; at times the women felt they couldn't have got through without that support.

Crisis support may seem an odd thing to include as one component, when all rape counselling is seen as 'crisis intervention'. There is a time though that dealing with actual crises is a very specific situation. Crisis interaction took place when women contacted the RCC feeling out of control and asked to be calmed down or talked through whatever was going on. It did not necessarily include the first call, even if this was in the immediate post-rape situation, but was a reflection of the panic moments many women experienced in coping. In particular, a woman can experience 'flashbacks', where she feels that it is happening again, or that her fear is so strong she can visualise her rapist(s). At these times, crisis support was used to help the woman ground herself in the present and so deal with her history.

Someone to talk to sums it up. Here, counselling was not seen as a woman's only or main source of support, but contact with the RCC was reassuring and acted as a back-up to a woman's own life.

Advice rarely occurred alone and was often in connection with 'back-up' support. Again it is self-evident. The RCC had information and experience that women found useful and could not easily be gained elsewhere.

Counselling another involved only occurred twice in this study, but did make a considerable difference for the raped woman herself. For the two young women, it was their mothers (main support for their daughters) who were also given specific support by an RCC counsellor. The emphasis was on giving the mothers space to get their own feelings out, and to explore ways of best helping their daughters through the victimisation process. There were other occasions when friends or relatives would make contact to ask how best they could help, or to let us know what was happening, and this was a part of the crucial role that those close to a woman who is raped can play. There was also recognition that the rape can produce a crisis for others apart from the woman who is raped.

If counselling took place *alongside other therapy*, then it was part of an acknowledgement that counselling focusing on the rape directly had its limitations and could not provide all the support needed all the time. When it worked best, the situation had clear components. Firstly, the desire to combine therapy and counselling came from the woman herself. Secondly, both therapist and counsellor were happy with the arrangement. Thirdly, no contact was made between the counsellor and therapist other than through the woman herself. In this way, she and she alone controlled what was said and to whom.

Practical help was asked for when problems apart from the rape could be dealt with. Housing, social security and social services contacts were all issues which women at times asked the RCC for help with.

Finally, there were three situations where contact with the RCC was kept up by women at the same time as they *rejected support*. Each woman said that they did not want to work through their feelings, they wanted to forget. One called in a panic, asking for something to stop her thinking. Another would only ask for things to be done for her, and the third just felt she could neither cope with thinking about the rape, nor justify taking up my time.

Looking at the conselling contact in this study, it is clear that women may ask for a wide range of actions and responses from others while dealing with rape. The counsellors at the RCC were focused on the fact of rape and set up to offer support. For a friend or relative, the position is less clear. Many people feel that the only answer to a woman who has been raped and has confided the fact, is to get them in touch with someone who can 'deal with it'. This study shows that one thing women may need is for her friends and relatives to help her deal with it, and to take it on for themselves. The next section is addressed to anyone who might be called upon to provide support for a woman who has been raped.

GIVING SUPPORT

At a police academy in the US, one trainee officer I spoke to said that he hated dealing with rape cases because he could never look a woman who'd been raped in the face. His concern was that his feeling of shame and helplessness would be seen by her as disgust. It is a rare human being who has that level of insight into their own effect on the feelings of others. One of the most common phrases used by people around raped women, however supportive they would like to be, is 'I don't know what to do.'

Charlotte's mother didn't know what to do as her daughter's rape contributed to a spiralling crisis. It was to her mother she returned after the rape, but Charlotte's presence was very disturbing to the whole family. Her mother was the one who used the RCC for support, never quite giving up on her daughter but being able to do little more than wait for the next crisis to hit. What she knew she could not do was to take out her own growing frustration on Charlotte herself. In many ways, the mother was caught up and victimised by the daughter's rape. **Diana**'s father, on the other hand, thought he knew exactly what to do when he was told she had been raped. He took over in discussions with the police, told her what she should be doing and feeling, and made his own distress central to everything. Her mother went hysterical. Diana's own control wavered when faced with her father's take over of her anger and her mother's take over of her distress. Luckily, friends who were closer to her, and with her more often, provided the support for Diana's own actions which was really needed.

However tempting it is to rush into 'doing something', the first lesson anyone who is with a raped woman must learn is – don't take over. Rape shows just how terrifying it can be to have someone else control your life. The well-meaning interference of friends and relatives can feel almost as frightening to a woman who is struggling to work out what happened and how she will cope. Having someone to phone the police, make appointments, help sort out housing or explain to the children, can help a great deal. If a woman asks for help, or we begin our help with 'Would you like me to . . .' means the difference between doing what a woman wants (and leaving her in control) and doing what we think is best.

As the police cadet noted, a woman who has been raped may well be very sensitive to others' responses to her, especially if she herself feels guilty or changed by the rape. A woman may either fear disbelief or a change in someone's attitude to them.

Patience contacted the RCC when she heard about it even though she had been raped years earlier. She felt that someone would at last believe her, after dismissive attitudes from her parents, a therapist and her husband. **Enid** was actually surrounded by people who both believed what had happened and believed in her, but she felt that the rape had changed her and she was no longer worth their attention or care.

There is a fine line here between needing to accept the reality of rape for a woman, and saying that it has not 'spoilt' her, and recognising that she feels different. It may help to keep in mind that the rape has taken away trust in the everyday security of life, and that it has made a drastic difference to how a woman will view her situation. It is not the woman herself who has changed, not her personality, but her understanding of herself in relation to the world. One young woman said she missed her innocence, and perhaps that's where the change is centred. Women will often say they fear the look of shock and disgust when telling someone about the rape. Shock and concern is a different face completely, and comes from accepting both the truth of rape and the feelings of women who have experienced it.

Having said that, however, there are reactions which can cause additional distress, even when they are rooted in acceptance and empathy.

Sara, for example, found her boyfriend's anger at the rapists frightening in itself. His rage and desire to do something reminded her of the violence the rapists had shown towards her. When he understood this, and got his own rage under control, she could relax. **Alice** found herself in a situation common to many women. Knowing her rapist well, the problem for her was other people knowing both her and the man who raped her, and how they handled this. However difficult the situation is for those others, to watch your friends and relatives joking around with the man who raped you can be either intolerable or unavoidable. Alice and her partner chose to separate themselves off, others couldn't. **Bea** and her partner chose to act as if nothing had happened when around the family, because they did not want a family split. **Anni** and her partner chose to split the rapist off from their friends because they could not face having him around.

What was essential in any situation is that those on the woman's 'side' (and with rape involved there are sides to take) asked the women what they wanted them to do – the decision, however it worked out, was in the hands of the raped women themselves.

One other situation, which did not come up in this study but which has in other counselling situations, is the fear response of others around the woman who has been raped. Having to deal with friends whose reaction to the rape has been to panic about their own security is very difficult. We cannot ask of ourselves that our own fears and feelings are totally submerged around a friend who has been raped, but it helps no-one to spread the feeling of crisis and being out of control. This situation is one where the involvement of someone from outside, who can provide space for all involved to deal with their feelings, can be most helpful.

Although women can have problems getting the support they need from another woman, there are specific issues brought up when men are asked for or want to offer support. Let's be honest, it is the general lack of male ability to understand or care about rape which makes the feminist response so important as support for raped women. Women will often prefer women medical or counselling staff when dealing with intimate physical contact and feelings. It is part of women's history that we have turned to each other in times of both joy and pain. However divisive society can get, we know we support each other. But, in a heterosexual relationship, the most intimate contact is with a male partner. Many such couples will proudly say they are each other's best friends as well as lovers. Male friends and relatives in this study were at times a problem, but at other times invaluable support. Rape can interest, frighten or excite any of us, but for men, the only knowledge they have of it is likely to be from the rapists' viewpoint, and this can confuse their response. The following comments are drawn in part from talking to men involved with the women in this study, and in part from wider counselling experience.

The first response from a man told about a rape by a woman close to him, is likely to be a stunned panic. He will know that he is being asked for support and comfort, but may find it difficult to deal with, especially if he is not used to fulfilling that role. Equally, he too has grown up in a world where rape is known about and may well feel a mixture of concern, anger and guilt – that another man can commit rape reflects on his own masculinity. The tendency for men (and some women) is to respond to a request for support with 'what you should do is . . .'. Action, or informing others, is a more comfortable response than accepting that there may be nothing that can be done other than say, in whatever way, 'I'm here'. The most difficult thing for any of us may well be to sit and let a woman cry, but if that is what is needed, it is the only thing to do. (Let me spell this out, because it is a common issue. To let someone cry is not to ignore them, or sit in embarrassed silence a safe distance apart from them. Giving someone space to let their feelings out means to focus on them, to stay in touch, to be thinking about them and showing your concern. It is not easy.)

Whatever a man understands about rape, the feeling will be communicated in an intimate relationship. For men it is often only women they will talk to about feelings. The heterosexual couple is supposed to be the one and only place for intimacy of act and feeling. However, when a woman has been raped, she may not want or need to be involved in an honest discussion about the feelings of her partner, to know how badly the rape has affected him. On the other hand, not dealing with his feelings will still leave atmospheres, vague feelings that something has changed. This can grow and undermine the potential support.

Where there is fear that the woman may have enjoyed rape, men must see that their own perception, from the outside, may well be of a sexual act, but that is not what the woman experienced. Rape, to someone who has not experienced it, can be thought of as sexual. Sex and violence are linked in social understanding. It may well be then that a sexual partner does find the idea of rape stimulating, and finds that feeling disturbing. Asking if a woman has enjoyed rape is like asking whether we would enjoy being beaten up. What has happened is an assault which used sex as a weapon, and the assailant was totally absorbed in his own experience. Men may rarely experience rape, but fear of having control taken away, of being overpowered, of being hurt, are all part of situations anyone can experience, and it may be worthwhile for a man to draw on these experiences in understanding what has happened to a woman he cares about.

The feeling of possessiveness, of ownership of a partner, is perhaps more difficult to deal with, as the social basis for the 'couple' is ownership of a sort. We know that, on a political level, rape in wartime has been used to engender feelings of humiliation in men at the rape of 'their' women, and such thinking feeds into our everyday, personal lives. The problem lies still with the view of rape as a sexual act, and of women as sexual objects. Perhaps a refocus on women as friends – on the whole relationship – helps here, for no-one would really be stimulated or made jealous by the idea of a friend being hurt.

Rape does threaten men's personal and sexual identity, not in the same way as for women, but through men's ability to be supportive. A man who regards rape as sex and exciting and thinks it OK to feel that their property has been spoilt, is incapable of giving support, and is unlikely to think of it. The ability to feel for another person is what makes the difference. The really selfish male, hooked into masculinity as a replacement for a personality, is too close to the rapist to be able to help. The hope lies in the ones who care and want to help.

One problem is that there may be little help or support available for such men. There has been some work advising male professionals on how to give support to women (Silverman, 1977), but work with male friends and relatives is sparse (Silverman, 1978). The Rape Crisis Centres are approached by men themselves, or may be asked to help by women, but it may not be the most appropriate source for support. RCCs are geared to the needs of women, and are a small enough resource. There are men's support groups, which have the advantage of challenging the assumption that women are the repository of all tender loving care. Men supporting each other, and challenging the myths of rape for themselves, seems a valuable move. Male professionals can offer the same kind of empathy to other men as women offer to each other.

Overall, the message to others who want to be supportive of a woman who has been raped is that to be there, to ask what is needed of you and do it, and to allow the woman to cope for herself, provides the basis for the support the women in this study found most helpful. It is also worth acknowledging that rape can be a crisis for more than the woman who experiences it directly. This is another example of the way that rape as an experience has ripples of response right through a woman's life and others involved with her, and how others may need support to work through their feelings, in order to be able to give support. The ability to feel is what makes the difference.

AND, IN THE END . . .

Listening to women shows rape not as a single act with one cause or meaning, but as a single term which covers a multitude of ways of abusing power and causing pain. To women who have experienced it, the act of rape is a denial of their right to self-control. It can feel like a punishment for some assumed wrong. Sometimes the wrong may be simply existing, according to the rapist anyway. Coping with rape means struggling to resume control, to deal with the anger and fear that victimisation produces, and learning to feel safe again. To all women, rape is a threat. It hangs over us whether we try to conform to the feminine ideal or whether we choose a different path for our existence. Some women may deny that it could happen to them, some will blame the victims in an attempt to distance themselves from rape. Some men will encourage this distancing, either to perpetuate the fear that is produced in women, or because they cannot accept the role which men assume in becoming rapists. Some men are ashamed of rape and angry that other men can consider it. For everyone, rape is a slur on the society it occurs within.

The connections

When the Women's Movement began to give space to women's experiences and feminism provided a view of rape, what emerged was an act which is rooted in the everyday, not a rare occurrence. Feminists did not deny that it was sick or evil, but pointed to the attitudes and structures which helped to perpetuate rape as an extreme example of the social contempt shown to women. The treatment of women as property, as adornments, and as objects, are old tales to feminists, ideas still shrugged off by the conservative minded. Inequality is no less real because we have been arguing about it for thousands of years. The links have been made between sexual violence in pornography, the selling of women and sex in advertising and other imagery, domestic violence, rape and child sexual abuse. It is attitudes and beliefs which produce all manifestations of sexism, and provide the connections between the many faces of exploitation.

Does rape constitute a crime?

Society's response to women has been dismissive and blaming, somewhat like the rapists'. This was and is reflected in the treatment of rape as a crime. There has been some improvement in the treatment of women by the police and criminal justice system. In the US this was a direct response to the feminist challenge; in the UK this will be denied. There is one immovable problem in treating rape as a crime which will always stand in the way of UK reforms. Once an act of rape becomes part of the legal process, the woman becomes a prosecution witness, a passive reporter of her experience. One woman in this study broke down in court and the judge snapped 'I will not have hysterical young women in my court.' Her head shot up and she returned 'well, don't try rape cases then'. She had a point. For a woman struggling to make sense of her experience and cope with her feelings, the attitude and distancing of the legal system may not be best for her personal progress. The counter-argument is always that only by reporting rape will society learn to take it seriously. We are in that case asking women to put their social conscience, the good of all women, in higher regard than their own recovery. We are asking more of ourselves than society as a whole is willing to do for us.

When looking at women's responses to rape as involving rational decision-making, that first decision of who to tell and why becomes crucial. In deciding whether or not to involve the police, women are making a personal comment on the social definition of rape as a crime, and how that crime is really dealt with. When considered from the point of view of what is best for a raped woman, questions emerge: Is to treat rape as a crime the most appropriate response that society can make? For whose benefit is it done? What more can be done? One crucial question which often emerges, sometimes months or years after the rape, is: if I don't call the rape a crime, how can I punish or define the rapist(s)? It is the question, multiplied, which really started the Anti-Rape Campaign.

Feminism and the future of an Anti-Rape Campaign

The Women's Movement reflected, on a political level, the personal experiences of women. The question of what could be done about rape was asked in both fear and anger. The Rape Crisis Centres, self-defence, community education and aware-ness projects, support groups, vigilante and revenge squads, police and professional training programmes, shelters and WORDS, all contained both the anger needed to say 'this cannot go on ignored', and the fear which also said 'we have to do something'. Women's need to regain control was equally re-flected in the actions, as the Women's Movement saw that both the action and the understanding behind it were needed to really combat at least the effects of rape.

If the anger of the Movement at times came out in ways which disturbed or alienated the general public, it was not surprising

— the general public needed upsetting out of the complacency which had permeated common understanding of rape. The anger of women who had learned about rape fed into the challenge thrown out to society to set its house in order, end discrimination of women and end its collusion in abuse. What was and is a more difficult problem for the Anti-Rape Campaign is the fear of rape which knowledge has engendered. Fear of rape is the central feeling which separates out an understanding based on the rapists' view and one based on the view of those who could be victimised. A rapist sees nothing to fear in rape, but a woman conscious of being a women sees plenty. It seemed impossible to learn about rape without learning about fear too, and the Anti-Rape Campaign did learn it, focused on it, and passed it on. At times, instead of awareness which could be used constructively, what we learned was a restricting truth. I sense now in the Women's Movement as a whole a fearful preoccupation with victimisation. This is not the whole story which comes from women's experiences, and is certainly not the only thing reflected in the accounts of women here. To a great extent, the Anti-Rape Campaign and the women themselves focused on surviving and changing. We must not lose that side of our response to rape.

There are questions still to be asked about rape, never mind the questions never answered. Tinkering with the legislation doesn't answer the question of whether rape constitutes a crime. From what we know, we still can wonder how real the change in attitude of the legal process is to rape and raped women, and how far the legal practitioners would go in calling what we know of as rape, a crime. Equally, if feminism is saying that rape is rooted in the everyday, where does the crime begin? There still are questions about the feminist understanding and response to rape: Is there more we can do? Is the support we have given enough, or completely appropriate? How do we make feminism a critique of victimisation, a perspective on change, rather than a victim perspective? And what of men? How far do we leave the responsibility for dealing with rapists and the causes of rape with them? How far can we rely on them? What could they do to change themselves?

We can be side-tracked into trying to 'prove' that pornography encourages rape, or deflected into debates on the idea of pornography as free speech, or whether images of women as 'available' exploit the viewer or the viewed. We may have to answer questions about the problems faced by men who have been sexually abused by women, and know that we question in turn the motives of those who cannot discuss violence against women without trying to trivialise it, or deflect it. We may have to face those who insist on making rape a joke, and know that it is done at times to annoy or bait us, and at times in unthinking ignorance. Just as rape itself is a show of contempt and anger at women's existence, then the contempt shown to feminism is also a sign of the disturbed feelings of those who wish to change nothing, who have a vested interest in women staying just where they are, who are ultimately on the side of the rapists.

It was said at the beginning that ending rape was an aim no-one could reasonably expect the Women's Movement to achieve. This may be true, but after a decade of work those involved can at least now imagine a world without it. Peggy Reeves Sanday (1981), in an anthropological study of 'rape prone' and 'rape free' societies, described the basis of a society free of rape. There is no obvious hierarchy of status between women and men, even if there are differences in tasks taken on; sex is non-competitive and non-possessive; discussion is welcome but argument is seen as noise and offensive to the environment. Reading through the fiction and the reality of feminist understanding, what emerges is a world of absences. There would be no status inequality giving any man any opportunity to see any woman as his inferior and exploitable; no structures such as marriage which hold one person to be the property of another; no self-interest but an acceptance of our responsibility to each other; no objectification of women as a group; no sexism, no racism, and perhaps no capitalism either. The more cynical, angry or ironic would add 'no men', but otherwise the hope is there that men too can change. Ultimately the test of the theory of what rape is and why it happens lies in ending rape, in finding out what has gone from society when we have changed it enough to see what is no longer there to encourage and support rape.

In the meantime, the phones are still ringing. . . .

BIBLIOGRAPHY

Abel, Gene (1977) 'The components of rapists' sexual arousal', *Archives of General Psychology*, vol. 34, August, pp. 895–903.

Acker, Joan (1980) 'Women and stratification: a review of recent literature', *Contemporary Sociology*, January, pp. 25–39.

Acker, Joan, Barry, Kate and Esseveld, Joke (1983) 'Objectivity and truth: problems in doing feminist research', *Women's Studies International Forum*, vol. 6, no. 4, pp. 423–35.

Albin, Rochelle S. (1977) 'Psychological studies of rape', *Signs*, vol. 3, no. 2, pp. 423–35.

Alder, Christine (1986) 'An exploration of self-reported sexually aggressive behavior', *Crime and Delinquency*, vol. 126, no. 1, February, pp. 306–31.

Amir, Menachim (1971) *Patterns in Forcible Rape*, University of Chicago Press, Chicago.

Anger, Jane (1974) 'Her protection for women', in Goulianos, J. (ed.) *By A Woman Writ*, New English Library, London.

Archer, John and Lloyd, Barbara (1982) *Sex and Gender*, Penguin Books, London.

Ardener, Shirley (1978) *Defining Females*, Croom Helm, London.

Atkeson, Beverley, Calhoun, Karen S., Resick, Patricia A. and Ellis, Elizabeth M. (1982) 'Victims of rape: repeated assessment of depressive symptoms', *Journal of Consulting and Clinical Psychology*, vol. 50, no. 1, pp. 96–102.

Babcock, B. A. (1973) 'Women and the criminal law', *American Criminal Law Review*, vol. 11, no. 2, Introduction.

Backhouse, Constance and Cohen, Leah (1978) *The Secret Oppression: Sexual Harassment of Working Women*, Macmillan, Toronto.

Baker Miller, Jean (ed.) (1973) *Psychoanalysis and Women*, Penguin Books, London.

Baker Miller, Jean (1979) *Towards a New Psychology of Women*, Penguin Books, London.

Bardwick, Judith M. (1972) *Readings on the Psychology of Women*, Harper & Row, New York.

Barnes, Josephine (1967) 'Rape and other sexual offences', *British Medical Journal*, 29 April, pp. 293–5.

Barrett, Michele and McIntosh, Mary (1982) *The Anti-Social Family*, Verso Editions, London.

Barry, David and Ciccone, J. R. (1975) 'Use of Depo Provera in the treatment of aggressive sexual offenders', *Bulletin of the American Academy of Psychiatry and Law*, vol. 3, no. 3, pp. 179–4.

Barry, Kathleen (1979) *Female Sexual Slavery*, Discus/Avon Books, New York.

Bart, Pauline (1975) 'Unalienating abortion, demystifying depression and restoring rape victims', paper presented to the American Psychiatric Association.

Bart, Pauline (1975) 'Rape doesn't end with a kiss', *Viva*, June.

de Beavoir, Simone (1969) *The Second Sex*, New English Library, London.

Becker, Howard S. (1967) 'Whose side are we on?' *Social Problems*, vol. 14, no. 3, pp. 239–48.

Bouchier, David (1983) *The Feminist Challenge*, MacMillan Press, London.

Brake, Mike (ed.) (1982) *Human Sexual Relations*, Penguin Books, London.

Brittan, Arthur (1984) *Sexism, Racism and Oppression* Blackwell, New York.

Brodsky, Annette (1973) 'The consciousness raising group as a model in therapy for women', *Psychotherapy: Theory, Research and Practice*, vol. 10.

Brodsky, Stanley L., Klemmack, Susan H., Skinner, Linda J., Bender, Lynn Z. and Polyson, Alexia M. K. (1977/8) *Sexual Assault: A Literature Analysis*, Centre for Correctional Psychology, Report No. 33.

Brodsky, Stanley L. and Klemmack, Susan H. (1977) *Blame Models and Assailant Research*, Research Paper, University of Alabama.

Brodyaga, Lisa (ed.) (1975) *Rape and its Victims: A Report*, National Institute of Law Enforcement and Criminal Justice, Washington DC.

Brownmiller, Susan (1975) *Against Our Will: Men, Women and Rape*, Secker and Warburg, London.

Burgess, Ann W. and Holmstrom, Lynda L. (1974) *Rape: Victims of Crisis*, Brady.

Burgess, Ann W. and Holmstrom, Lynda L. (1976) 'Coping behavior of the rape victim', *American Journal of Psychology*, vol. 133, no. 4, pp. 413–17.

Burgess, Ann W. and Holmstrom, Lynda L. (1978) *The Victim of Rape: Institutional Reaction*, Wiley, New York.

Burt, M. R. and Katz, B. L. (1975) 'Rape, robbery and burglary: responses to actual and feared criminal victimisation, with special focus on women and the elderly', *Victimology*, vol. 10, nos 1–4, pp. 325–58.

Calhoun, L. G., Selby, J. W. and Warring, L. J. (1976) 'Social perceptions of the victim's causal role in rape', *Human Relations*, vol. 29, no. 6, pp. 517–26.

Calmas, W. E. (1965) *Fantasies of the Mother–Son Relationship of the Rapist and the Pedophile*, PhD Thesis, Boston University.

Campbell, Beatrix (1974) 'Sexuality and submission', *Red Rag*, no. 5, pp. 12–15.

Carbary, Lorraine (1974) 'Treating terrified victims', *Journal of Practical Nursing*, February, p. 22.

Caringella-MacDonald, S. (1985) 'The comparability in sexual and nonsexual assault case treatment: did statute change meet the objective?, *Crime and Delinquency*, vol. 31, no. 2, pp. 206–22.

Chapman, Jane and Gates, Margaret (1978) *The Victimisation of Women*, Sage, Beverly Hills, Calif.

Chappell, Duncan, Geis, Gilbert and Fogarty, Faith (1974) 'Research notes: forcible rape bibliography', *Journal of Criminal Law and Criminology*, vol. 65, no. 2, pp. 248–63.

Clark, J. H. and Zarrow, M. X. (1971) 'The influence of copulation on time of ovulation in women', *American Journal of Obstetrics and Gynaecology*, vol. 109, no. 7, pp. 1083–5.

Clark, Lorenne and Lewis, Debra (1977) *Rape: The Price of Coercive Sexuality*, The Women's Press, Toronto.

Clarke, L. G. (ed.) (1979) *The Sexism of Social and Political Theory*, University of Toronto Press.

Cohen, Murray L., Garafalo, Ralph, Bouchier, Richard and Seghorn, Theo (1971) 'The psychology of rapists', *Seminars in Psychiatry*, vol. 3, no. 3, August, pp. 307–27.

Cohen, Murray L. and Bouchier, Richard (1972) 'Misunderstandings about sex criminals', *Sexual Behavior*, vol. 2, no. 3, pp. 57–62.

Connell, Noreen and Wilson, Cassandra (eds) (1974) *Rape: The First Sourcebook for Women*, New American Library, New York.

Coote, Anna and Campbell, Beatrix (1982) *Sweet Freedom: The Struggle for Women's Liberation*, Picador/Pan/Basil Blackwell, London.

Coote, Anna and Gill, Tess (1975) *The Rape Controversy*, National Council for Civil Liberties Pamphlet, London.

Coyner, Sandra (1977) 'Women's liberation and sexual liberation', in Libby, R. and Whitehurst, R. *Marriage and Alternatives*, Scott Foresman & Co, Illinois.

Daly, Mary (1979) *Gyn/Ecology*, The Women's Press, London.

Davis, Angela (1975) 'Joanna Little: the dialectics of rape', *Forum*, June.

Deegan, M. and Hill, M. (eds) (1987) *Women and Symbolic Interaction*, Allen and Unwin, London.

Delin, Bart (1978) *The Sex Offender*, Beacon Press, Boston.

Denning, M. and Eppy, A. (1981) 'The sociology of rape', *Sociology and Social Research*, vol. 65, no. 4, pp. 357–81.

Dennismore, Dana (1970) 'On the temptation to be a beautiful object', in Stambler, S. (ed.) *Women's Liberation*, Ace Books, New York, pp. 13–16.

Dering, Sarah (1979) *Some Thoughts on the Reading of Women's Studies in Universities*, Workshop discussion paper, Women's Research and Resources Conference Centre, Bradford.

Dobash, R. and Dobash, R. (1979) *Violence Against Wives: A Case Against the Patriarchy*, Free Press, New York.

Drapkin, Israel and Viano, Emilio (eds) (1975) *Victimology: A New Focus*, vols 1–6, Lexington Books/DC Heath & Co., Lexington, Mass.; London.

Dwayne-Smith, M. *et al.* (1985) 'Poverty, inequality and theories of forcible rape', *Crime and Delinquency*, vol. 31, no. 2, pp. 295–305.

Dworkin, Andrea (1974) *Woman Hating*, E. P. Dutton, New York.

Dworkin, Andrea (1983) *Right Wing Women*, Women's Press, London.

Dworkin, Andrea (1984) *Pornography*, Women's Press, London.

East, Norwood (1955) *Sexual Offenders*, Delisle, London.

Edwards, Alison (1976) *Rape, Racism and the White Women's Movement: An Answer to Susan Brownmiller*, Sojourner Truth Organisation, pamphlet.

Edwards, Susan (1979) 'Female sexuality: passivity or precipitation?', Paper presented to the British Psychological Society Conference, Division of Legal and Criminological Psychology, December, London.

Edwards, Susan (1981) *Female Sexuality and the Law*, Martin Robertson, Oxford.

Eisenstein, Hester (1984) *Contemporary Feminist Thought*, Counterpoint/Unwin Paperbacks, London.

Eisenstein, Zillah (1979) *Capitalism, Patriarchy and the Case for Socialist Feminism*, Monthly Review Press, New York.

Ernst, Sheila and Goodison, Lucy (1984) *In Our Own Hands: A Book of Self-Help Therapy*, Women's Press, London.

Farley, Lyn (1978) *Sexual Shakedown*, Melbourne House, London.

Feldman-Summers, Shirley (1976a) 'Perceptions of victims and defendants in criminal assault cases', *Criminal Justice and Behavior*, vol. 3, no. 2, pp. 135–50.

Feldman-Summers, Shirley (1976b) 'Conceptual and empirical issues associated with rape', in Viano, E. (ed.) *Victims and Society*, Visage Press, Washington DC.

Feldman-Summers, Shirley and Ashworth, Clarke (1981) 'Factors related to intentions to report a rape', *Journal of Social Issues*, vol. 37, no. 4, pp. 53–70.

Feminist Alliance Against Rape (1976) 'Black women and rape', *Newsletter*, November/December.

Feminist Alliance Against Rape (1976) 'National news notes', *Newsletter*, September/October.

Feminist Anthology Collective (1981) *No Turning Back*, Women's Press, London.

Field, Hubert S. (1978) 'Attitudes towards rape: a comparative analysis of police, rapists, crisis counsellors and citizens', *Journal of Personality and Social Psychology*, vol. 36, no. 2, pp. 156–79.

Field, Hubert S. and Barnett, Nora J. (1977) 'Forcible rape: an updated bibliography', *Journal of Criminal Law and Criminology*, March.

Figes, Eva (1976) 'Rape: war zone of sexual politics', *Psychology Today*, May, pp. 13–19.

Findlay, Barbara (1974) 'The cultural context of rape', *Women Lawyers Journal*, vol. 60, Fall, pp. 199–207.

Fisher, Gary and Rivlin, Ephraim (1971) 'Psychological needs of rapists', *British Journal of Criminology*, vol. 11, pp. 182–4.

Fox, Greer Litton (1977) 'Nice girls: social control of women through a value construct', *Signs*, vol. 2, no. 4, pp. 805–17.

Frazer, John (1976) *Violence in the Arts*, Cambridge University Press, Cambridge.

Freeman, Jo (1970) *The Social Construction of the Second Sex*, Know Inc., Pittsburg, PA.

Gagnon, J. H. and Simon, W. (1974) *Sexual Conduct* Hutchinson, London.

Galvin, Jim (1985) 'Rape: a decade of reform', *Crime and Delinquency*, vol. 31, no. 2, pp. 163–8.

Garret, T. B. and Wright, R. (1985) 'Wives of rapists and incest offenders', *Journal of Sex Research*, vol. 11, no. 2, pp. 148–57.

Gebhard, Paul, Gagnon, J. H., Pomeroy, W. and Christerson, C. (1965) *Sex Offenders*, Harper & Row, New York.

Geis, Gilbert (1971) 'Group sexual assaults', *Medical Aspects of Human Sexuality*, vol. 5, no. 5, May, pp. 101–14.

Geis, Gilbert and Chappell, Duncan (1971) 'Forcible rape by multiple offenders', *Abstracts on Criminology and Penology*, vol. 11, no. 4, pp. 431–6.

Geis, Robley and Geis, Gilbert (1977) 'Anonymity in rape cases', *Justice of the Peace*, vol. 141, 21 May, pp. 293–4.

Geller, Sheldon H. (1977) 'The sexually assaulted female: innocent victim or temptress', *Canada's Mental Health*, vol. 25, no. 1, pp. 26–9.

Gelles, Richard (1977) 'Power, sex and violence: the case of marital rape', *Family Co-ordinator*, vol. 26, no. 4, pp. 339–47.

Gerzon, Mark (1982) *A Choice of Heroes*, Houghton Mifflin Co., Boston.

Gibbons, Donald C. (1984) 'Forcible rape and sexual violence – NCCD Research Review', *Journal of Research in Crime and Delinquency*, vol. 21, no. 3, pp. 251–67.

Gillespie, Fulton (1976) 'The Cambridge rapist', *Verdict*, vol. 1, no. 2, pp. 6–19.

Gissing, George (1980) *The Odd Women*, Virago Modern Classics, London.

Glaser, B. and Strauss, A. (1975) *The Discovery of Grounded Theory*, Aldine Pub Co..

Goffman, Erving (1963) *Stigma*, Penguin Books, London.

Golden Reid, M. and Messner, Steven (1987) 'Dimensions of racial inequality and rates of violent crime', *Criminology*, vol. 25, no. 1, pp. 525–42.

Gordon, Linda (1977) *Woman's Body, Woman's Right*, Penguin Books, London.

Gornick, Vivian (1971) *Women in Sexist Society*, Basic Books, New York.

Gornick, Vivian (1978) *Essays in Feminism*, Harper & Row, New York.

Greer, Germaine (1976) 'What is rape?' *The New Review*, vol. 2, no. 22, 22 January.

Griffin, Susan (1971) 'Rape: the all American crime', *Ramparts*, vol. 10, no. 3, pp. 2–8.

Griffin, Susan (1979) *Rape: The Power of Consciousness*, Harper & Row, New York.

Groth, Nicholas 'The adolescent sexual offender and his prey', *International Journal of Offender Therapy and Comparative Criminology*, vol. 21, no. 3, pp. 249–63.

Groth, Nicholas and Birbaum, Jean (1979) *Men Who Rape*, Plenum Press, New York.

Groth, Nicholas and Burgess, Ann W. (1977) 'Rape: a sexual deviation', *American Journal of Orthopsychiatry*, vol. 47, no. 3, July, pp. 400–6.

Groth, Nicholas and Burgess, Ann W. (1977) 'Sexual dysfunction during rape', *New England Journal of Medicine*, 6 October, pp. 764–6.

Hall, Ruth (1985) *Ask Any Woman*, Falling Wall Press, Bristol.

Hanisch, Carol (1972) 'The liberal takeover of women's liberation', in *Redstockings: Feminist Revolution*, New York, pp. 127–31.

Hanmer, J. and Maynard, M. (eds) (1987) *Women, Violence and Social Control*, MacMillan, London.

Hanmer, J. and Stanko, E. (1985) 'Stripping away the rhetoric of protection: violence to women, law and the state in Britain and the USA', *International Journal of the Sociology of Law*, vol. 13, no. 1, pp. 357–74.

Hayman, Charles R. (1971) 'Victimology of sexual assault', *Medical Aspects of Human Sexuality*, vol. 5, no. 10, pp. 152–61.

Hernton, Calina (1970) *Sex and Racism*, Paladin, London.

Hinch, R. (1985) 'Canada's new sexual assault laws: a step forward for women?', *Contemporary Crises*, vol. 9, no. 1, pp. 33–44.

Hite, Shere (1977) *The Hite Report*, Summit Books, London.

Holmes, Karen and Williams, Joyce (1978) *Problems and Pitfalls of Rape Victim Research*, Research working paper, Trinity University, San Antonio, Texas.

Hopkins, June (ed.) (1984) *Perspectives on Rape and Sexual Assault*, Harper & Row, London.

Horowitz, Lucy and Ferleger, Lou (1980) *Statistics for Social Change*, South End Press, Boston.

Howells, K. *et al.* (1984) 'Perceptions of rape in a British sample: effects of relationship, victim status, sex and attitudes to women', *British Journal of Social Psychology*, vol. 23, no. 1, pp. 35–40.

Inciardi, J. and Poitieger, A. (eds) (1978) *Violent Crime: Historical and Contemporary Issues*, Sage, London.

Kanin, E. J. and Parcell, S. R. (1977) 'Sexual aggression: a second look at the offended female', *Archives of Sexual Behavior*, vol. 6, no. 1, pp. 67–76.

Kardener, Sheldon H. (1975) 'Rape fantasies', *Journal of Religion and Health*, vol. 14, no. 1.

Katz, Sedelle and Mazur, Mary Ann (1979) *Understanding the Rape Victim*, Wiley/Interscience, New York.

Kelly, Liz (1988) *Surviving Sexual Violence*, Polity Press, Cambridge.

Kercher, Glen (1973) 'The reactions of convicted rapists to sexually explicit stimuli', *Journal of Abnormal Psychology*, vol. 81, pp. 46–50.

Kerr, Norbert L. *et al.* (1985) 'Effects of victim attractiveness, care and disfigurement on the judgements of American and British mock jurors', *British Journal of Social Psychology*, vol. 24, part 1, pp. 47–58.

Kilpatrick, Dean G., Resick, Patricia A. and Veronen, Lois J. (1981) 'Effects of rape experience: a longitudinal study', *Journal of Social Issues* vol. 37, no. 4, pp. 105–22.

Kirkpatrick, C. and Kanin E. (1957) 'Male sexual aggression on a university campus', *American Sociological Review*, vol. 22, pp. 52–8.

Koedt, Ann (1970) 'The myth of the vaginal orgasm', in Koedt, A., Levine, E. and Rapone, A. (eds) *Radical Feminism*, Quadrangle, New York.

Kollontai, Alexandra (1972) *Sexual Relations and the Class Struggle*, Falling Wall Press, Bristol.

Lafree, G. D. *et al.* (1985) 'Jurors' responses to victims' behavior and legal issues in sexual assault trials', *Social Problems*, vol. 32, no. 4, April, p. 389.

Lazarre, Jan (1981) *On Loving Men*, Virago, London.

Le Beau (1987) 'Patterns of stranger and serial rape offending: factors distinguishing apprehended and at large offenders', *Journal of Criminal Law and Criminology*, vol. 78, no. 2, pp. 309–26.

Leeds Revolutionary Feminist Group (1979) *Every Single Academic Feminist Owes Her Livelihood to the WLM*, Workshop discussion paper, Women's Research and Resources Centre Conference, Bradford.

Legrand, Camille (1973) 'Rape and rape laws: sexism in society and law', *California Law Review*, vol. 61, no. 3, pp. 919–41.

Leonard, Eileen B. (1982) *Women, Crime and Society*, Longman Inc., New York.

Lester, David (1975) *Unusual Sexual Behavior: The Standard Deviations*, CC Thomas, Illinois.

Livingston, Sonia and Green, Gloria (1986) 'TV advertisements and the portrayal of gender', *British Journal of Social Psychology*, vol. 25, no. 2, pp. 149–54.

Lizotte, Alan J. (1985) 'The uniqueness of rape: reporting assaultive violence to the police', *Crime and Delinquency*, vol. 31, no. 2, pp. 169–90.

London Rape Crisis Centre (1984) *Sexual Violence*, Women's Press, London.

Luker, Kristin (1975) *Taking Chances: Abortion and the Decision not to Contracept*, University of California Press, Berkley, Calif.

McCombie, Sharon (1975) *Characteristics of Rape Victims seen in Crisis Intervention*, Master of Social Work Thesis, Smith College School of Social Work.

MacDonald, John M. (1971) *Rape Offenders and Their Victims*, CC Thomas, Illinois.

MacNamara, Donald E. and Sagarin, Edward (1977) *Sex Crime and the Law*, Free Press, New York.

Meade, Marian (1973) *Bitching*, Garnstone Press, London.

Medea, Andra and Thompson, Kathleen (1974) *Against Rape*, Noonday Press, New York.

Midlarsky, Elizabeth (1977) *Research On Rape: Some Methodological Considerations*, Research Paper, University of Detroit.

Millet, Kate (1971) *Sexual Politics*, Hart-Davis, London.

Millet, Kate (1973) *The Prostitution Papers*, Avon Books, New York.

Millman, M. and Moss, Kanter (1976) *Another Voice*, Doubleday, New York.

Mitchell, Juliet (1982) *Psychoanalysis and Feminism*, Penguin Books, London.

Mitchell, Juliet (1984) *Women: The Longest Revolution*, Virago, London.

Morgan, Robin (1970) *Sisterhood is Powerful*, Vintage Books, New York.

Nails, D. (1983) 'Social-scientific sexism: Gilligan's mismeasure of man', *Social Research*, vol. 50, no. 3, pp. 643–64.

National Center for the Prevention and Control of Rape (1978) *Basic and Applied Studies*, Resumé of research projects funded 1976–8, National Rape Information Clearing House, March.

Notman, M. T. (1976) 'The rape victim: psychodynamic considerations', *American Journal of Psychology*, vol. 133, no. 4, pp. 408–13.

Oakley, Ann (1972) *Sex, Gender and Society*, Temple Smith with New Society, London.

Oakley, Ann (1985) *The Sociology of Housework*, Blackwell, Oxford.

O'Keefe, Nona, Brockopp, Karen and Chew, Esther (1986) 'Teen dating violence', *Social Work*, November/December, pp. 465–8.

Okin, Susan Moller (1979) *Women in Western Political Thought*, Princeton University Press, Princeton, NJ.

Parker, Tony (1969) *The Twisting Lane*, Panther Press, London.

Peters, Joseph F. (1975) *Social Psychiatric Study of Victims Reporting Rape*, paper presented to the American Psychiatry Association 128th Annual Meeting, Anaheim, May.

Pitch, T. (1985) 'Critical criminology, the construction of social problems and the question of rape', *International Journal of the Sociology of Law*, vol. 13, no. 1, pp. 35–46.

Pizzey, Erin (1974) *Scream Quietly . . .*, Penguin Books, London.

Plummer, Ken (1975) *Sexual Stigma*, Routledge & Kegan Paul, London.

Polk, Kenneth (1985) 'A comparative analysis of attrition of rape cases', *British Journal of Criminology*, vol. 25, no. 3, pp. 280–4.

Puppe, George (1935) *The Hymen: A Medico-Legal Study of Rape*, Physicians and Surgeons Press.

Radcliffe Richards, Janet (1980) *The Sceptical Feminist*, Routledge & Kegan Paul, London.

Radzinowicz, L. (1957) *Sexual Offences*, Macmillan, London.

Rape Counselling and Research Project (1977; 1978; 1982) *Rape Crisis Centre*: First Report; Second Report; Third Report.

Resick, Patricia A., Calhoun, Karen S., Atkeson, Beverley M. and Ellis, Elizabeth M. (1981) 'Social adjustments in victims of sexual assault', *Journal of Consulting and Clinical Psychology*, vol. 49, no. 5, pp. 705–12.

Reynolds, Janice (1972) 'Rape as social control', *Telos*, vol. 18, pp. 62–7.

Riger, Stephanie and Gordon, Margaret (1981) 'The fear of rape: a study in social control', *Journal of Social Issues*, vol. 37, no. 4, pp. 71–92.

Roberts, Helen (ed.) (1981) *Doing Feminist Research*, Routledge & Kegan Paul, London.

Robin, Gerald D. (1977) 'Forcible rape: institutionalised sexism in the criminal justice system', *Crime and Delinquency*, vol. 23, no. 2, pp. 137–53.

Rock, Paul (1973) *Deviant Behavior*, Hutchinson University Library.

Rohrbaugh, Joanna Bunker (1981) *Women: Psychology's Puzzle*, Abacus, Tunbridge Wells.

Roth, Nathan (1952) 'Factors in motivation of sexual offenders', *Journal of Criminal Law and Criminology*, vol. 42, pp. 631–5.

Roth, J. (1974) 'Care of the sick: professionalism v. love', *Social Science and Medicine*, vol. 1, no. 3, pp. 173–80.

Rowbotham, Sheila (1974) *Hidden From History*, Pluto Press, London.

Russell, Diana (1982) *Rape in Marriage*, Collier/MacMillan, New York.

Russianoff, Penelope (1981) *Women in Crisis*, Human Science Press.

Ryan, William (1976) *Blaming the Victim*, Vintage Books, New York.

Saffioti, Helieth (1978) *Women in Class Society*, Monthly Review Press, New York.

Sanday, Peggy Reeves (1981) 'The socio-cultural context of rape', *Journal of Social Issues*, vol. 37, no. 4, a special issue on rape.

Schneir, Miriam (ed.) (1972) *Feminism: The Essential Historical Writings*, Vintage/Random House, New York.

Schwartz, M. and Clear, T. R. (1980) 'Towards a new law on rape', *Crime and Delinquency*, vol. 26, no. 2, pp. 129–51.

Schwendinger, J. and Schwendinger, H. (1969) 'Rape myths: in legal, theoretical and everyday practice', *Crime and Social Justice*, no. 1, pp. 18–26.

Schwendinger, J. and Schwendinger, H. (1983) *Rape and Inequality*, Sage, London.

Scott, R. L. and Tetreault, L. A. (1987) 'Attitudes of rapists and other violent offenders towards women', *Journal of Social Psychology*, vol. 127, no. 4, pp. 375–80.

Sedley, Ann and Benn, Melissa (1982) *Sexual Harassment at Work*, National Council for Civil Liberties, Rights of Women Unit, London.

Shapiro, Rose (1970) 'Prisoner of Revlon', *The Leveller*, no. 37, April; reprinted in Feminist Anthology Collective *No Turning Back*, Women's Press, London (1981).

Silverman, Daniel (1977) 'First do no more harm: female rape victims and the male counsellor', *American Journal of Orthopsychiatry*, vol. 47, no. 1, pp. 91–6.

Silverman, Daniel (1978) 'Sharing the crisis of rape: counselling the mates and families of victims', *American Journal of Orthopsychiatry*, vol. 48, no. 1, pp. 166–73.

Simpson, Anthony E. (1986) 'The blackmail myth and the prosecution of rape and its attempt in 18th century London', *Journal of Criminal Law and Criminology*, vol. 77, no. 1, pp. 101–50.

Smart, Carol (1978) *Women, Sexuality and Social Control*, Routledge & Kegan Paul, London.

Solanis, Valerie (1971) *The SCUM Manifesto*, Olympia Press, London.

Soothill, K. and Jack, A. (1975) 'How rape is reported', *New Society*, 19 June.

Spender, Dale (1977) *Man Made Language*, Routledge & Kegan Paul, London.

Stambler, Sookie (ed.) (1970) *Women's Liberation: Blueprint for the Future*, Ace Books, New York.

Stanley, L. and Wise, S. (1983) *Breaking Out: Feminist Consciousness and Feminist Research*, Routledge & Kegan Paul, London.

Strauss, Anselm (1987) *Qualitative Analysis for Social Scientists*, Cambridge University Press, Cambridge.

Sutherland, D. and Scherl, S. (1970) 'Patterns of response among victims of rape', *American Journal of Orthopsychiatry*, vol. 40, no. 3, April, pp. 503–11.

Sykes, G. M. and Matza, D. (1957) 'Techniques of neutralisation: a theory of delinquency', *American Sociological Review*, vol. 22, pp. 664–70.

Symonds, Martin (1975) 'Victims of violence: psychological effects and aftereffects', *American Journal of Psychoanalysis*, vol. 35, no. 1, pp. 19–26.

Symonds, Martin (1976) 'The rape victim: psychological patterns of response', *American Journal of Psychoanalysis*, vol. 36, no. 1, pp. 27–34.

Taubman, S. (1986) 'Beyond the bravado: sex roles and the exploitative male, *Social Work*, vol. 31, no. 1, pp. 12–19.

Taylor, Laurie (1972) 'The significance and interpretation of replies to motivational questions: the case of sex offenders', *Sociology*, vol. 6, no. 1, pp. 23–39.

Tickner, Lisa (1976) 'Why not slip into something a little more comfortable?', *Spare Rib*, October, reprinted in *Spare Rib Reader*, Penguin, London (1982).

Vetterling-Braggin, M. (1981) *Sexist Language*, Littlefield Adams, New York.

Viano, Emilio (ed.) *Victims and Society*, Visage Press, Washington DC.

von Hentig, Hans (1979) *The Criminal and His Victim*, Schocken Books, New York.

Walmley, Roy (1980) 'Prosecution rates, sentencing practice and maximum penalties for sexual offences', in West D. J. (ed.) *Sex Offenders in the Criminal Justice System*, Cropwood Conference Series No. 12, Cambridge.

Walsh, Anthony (1986) 'Placebo justice: victim recommendations and offender sentences in sexual assault cases', *Journal of Criminal Law and Criminology*, vol. 77, no. 4, pp. 1126–41.

Wandor, Micheline (ed.) (1972) *The Body Politic*, Stage 1, London.

Warner, Marina (1976) *Alone of All Her Sex: The Myth and the Cult of the Virgin Mary*, Picador, London.

Warr, Mark (1985) 'Fear of rape among urban women', *Social Problems*, vol. 32, no. 3, February, pp. 238–50.

Weeks, J. (1981) *Sex, Politics and Society*, Longmans, London.

Weiss, Kurt and Borges, Sandra (1973) 'Victimology and rape: the case of the legitimate victim', *Issues in Criminology*, vol. 8, no. 2, pp. 71–115.

Werner, Arnold (1972) 'Rape: interruption of the therapeutic process by external stress', *Psychotherapy: Theory, Research and Practice*, vol. 9, no. 4, pp. 349–51.

West, Donald (1978) *Understanding Sexual Attacks*, Heinemann, London.

Whyte, William F. (1955) *Street Corner Society*, University of Chicago Press, Chicago.

Williams, J. E. (1984) 'Secondary victimisation: confronting public attitudes about rape', *Victimology*, vol. 9, no. 1, pp. 66–81.

Williams, Juanita H. (1977) *Psychology of Women*, W. W. Norton and Co., New York.

Wilson, Elizabeth (1983) *What Is To Be Done About Violence Against Women?*, Penguin Books, London.

Wright, Richard (1980) *Patterns of Rape in England*, PhD Thesis, Cambridge University.

Wyre, Ray (1986) *Women, Men and Rape*, Perry Publications, Oxford.

INDEX